best
hikes
with
dogs

NEW HAMPSHIRE & VERMONT

best
hikes
with
dogs

NEW HAMPSHIRE & VERMONT

Lisa Densmore

THE MOUNTAINEERS BOOKS

Dedication

To "Bravo," my Chesapeake Bay retriever who likes to hike as much as I do.

THE MOUNTAINEERS BOOKS
*is the nonprofit publishing arm of The Mountaineers Club, an organization
founded in 1906 and dedicated to the exploration, preservation, and
enjoyment of outdoor and wilderness areas.*

1001 SW Klickitat Way, Suite 201, Seattle, WA 98134

Published simultaneously in Great Britain by Cordee, 3a DeMontfort Street, Leicester,
England, LE1 7HD

Manufactured in the United States of America

Acquiring Editor: Cassandra Conyers
Project Editor: Laura Drury
Copy Editor: Jane Crosen
Cover and Book Design: The Mountaineers Books
Layout: Mayumi Thompson
Cartographer: Moore Creative Designs; Profiles: Judy Petry
Photographer: All photographs by the author

Cover photograph: *Bravo, a happy hiker*
Frontispiece: *Bravo on the summit of Mount Monroe*

Maps shown in this book were produced using National Geographic's
TOPO! software. For more information, go to *www.nationalgeographic.
com/topo*.

Library of Congress Cataloging-in-Publication Data
Densmore, Lisa Feinberg.
  Best hikes with dogs. New Hampshire & Vermont / Lisa Densmore.-- 1st ed.
    p. cm.
  Includes index.
  ISBN 0-89886-988-9 (pbk.)
  1. Hiking with dogs--New Hampshire--Guidebooks. 2. Hiking with dogs--Vermont--
Guidebooks. 3. Trails--New Hampshire--Guidebooks. 4. Trails--Vermont--Guidebooks.
5. New Hampshire--Guidebooks. 6. Vermont--Guidebooks. I. Title.
  SF427.455.D46 2005
  796.51'09742--dc22

CONTENTS

Part 3: Vermont

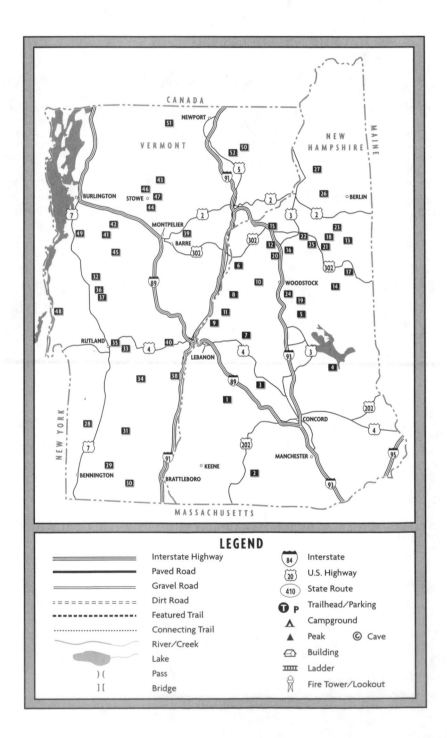

LEGEND

Interstate Highway	Interstate
Paved Road	U.S. Highway
Gravel Road	State Route
Dirt Road	Trailhead/Parking
Featured Trail	Campground
Connecting Trail	Peak Cave
River/Creek	Building
Lake	Ladder
Pass	Fire Tower/Lookout
Bridge	

HIKE SUMMARY TABLE

Trail	Hike 5 miles or less	Open summit	Mountain views	Fire tower or viewing platform*	Ledges or cliffs	Long ridge walk	River, lake, or pond	Waterfall	Dog-friendly shelter or campsite	Good for senior dogs	For fit dogs only
1. Lake Solitude–Mount Sunapee	•		•	•	•		•			•	
2. North Pack Monadnock	•	•	•	•		•				•	
3. Mount Kearsarge	•	•	•	•	•						
4. Mount Major	•	•	•		•						
5. Mount Percival–Mount Morgan Loop		•	•		•	•					
6. Black Mountain	•	•	•		•						•
7. Mount Cardigan	•	•	•	•	•			•		•	
8. Mount Cube		•	•				•		•		
9. Moose Mountain			•		•	•			•		
10. Mount Moosilauke		•	•						•		•
11. Smarts Mountain			•	•	•	•			•		•
12. Bridal Veil Falls	•				•		•	•	•	•	
13. Carter Dome–Mount Hight Loop		•	•		•	•	•				•
14. Mount Chocorua		•	•		•			•			•
15. Kilburn Crag	•		•		•					•	
16. Mount Lafayette		•	•		•	•	•				•
17. The Moats		•	•		•	•	•	•			•
18. Mount Monroe		•	•		•	•					•
19. Mount Osceola		•	•		•						
20. Mount Pemigewasset	•	•	•		•					•	
21. Mounts Pierce and Eisenhower		•	•		•	•		•			•
22. North Sugarloaf and Middle Sugarloaf	•	•	•		•		•		•		
23. Mount Washington		•	•	•	•	•	•				•
24. Welch Mountain–Dickey Mountain Loop	•	•	•		•	•					•
25. Mount Willard	•	•	•		•			•		•	

Trail	Hike 5 miles or less	Open summit	Mountain views	Fire tower or viewing platform*	Ledges or cliffs	Long ridge walk	River, lake, or pond	Waterfall	Dog-friendly shelter or campsite	Good for senior dogs	For fit dogs only
26. Mount Cabot–Unknown Pond Loop		●	●		●	●	●		●		●
27. North Percy	●	●	●		●						●
28. Mount Equinox			●		●						
29. Haystack Mountain	●	●	●		●					●	
30. Mount Olga	●		●	●					●	●	
31. Stratton Mountain–Stratton Pond Loop			●	●			●		●		●
32. Abbey Pond	●						●		●		
33. Killington Peak		●	●		●				●		●
34. Okemo (Ludlow) Mountain			●	●							
35. Pico Peak		●	●	●					●		
36. Pleiad Lake	●	●					●		●	●	
37. Silver Lake							●	●	●		
38. Mount Ascutney			●	●	●						
39. Spruce Mountain	●		●	●	●					●	
40. Mount Tom and The Pogue	●	●	●		●		●			●	
41. Burnt Rock Mountain		●	●		●	●					
42. Camels Hump		●	●		●				●		●
43. Mount Elmore	●		●	●	●				●	●	
44. Mount Hunger	●	●	●		●						●
45. Lincoln Gap–Appalachian Gap		●	●		●	●			●		●
46. Mount Mansfield		●	●		●	●			●		●
47. Stowe Pinnacle	●	●	●		●					●	
48. Mount Independence	●		●		●		●			●	
49. Mount Philo	●	●	●	●	●					●	
50. Bald Mountain	●		●	●					●	●	
51. Jay Peak	●	●	●		●					●	●
52. Mount Pisgah	●		●		●			●		●	

* Includes deck of summit hut

ACKNOWLEDGMENTS

Special thanks to the following people who have given their valuable expertise, opinions, and advice about hiking with dogs, not to mention encouragement about this book.

First, my family: My husband Jason and my son Parker, who not only accompanied me on a number of hikes while I was working on this book, but also held the household together while I stayed up night after night to write it; Martha Densmore, my mother-in-law, who lent me her camera so that I could bring professional-quality images from the trails to you; and my father-in-law, Ja Densmore, whose beautiful photos, knowledge of photography, and encouragement gave me the confidence to push the button again and again.

For their inspiration: Dan Nelson, author of the original book in this series, *Best Hikes with Dogs: Western Washington*. Without the gift of his book, his insight and his encouragement, I might never have written the first word of this book; and to Paige Boucher and Cathy Wiedemer, the P.R. team at Mountain Hardwear, who threw Dan and me together on a backcountry ski trip and have outfitted me for many of my recent mountain adventures, including the hikes in this book.

For their dog-hiking wisdom: Dr. Arleigh Reynolds, for his insights into the nutritional needs of working dogs; David Bumstead, a fellow dog-hiker who knows the best backpacking routes in the Whites with a pooch; Paul Kruse, "Leader of the Pack" at Ruff Wear for supplying my dog, Bravo, with everything he needs for the trail, and for letting me pick his brain about all aspects of dog gear; and Dr. Laurie DeMuth, the only veterinarian I know that hikes regularly with her dog, for educating me about the most common injuries dogs have on the trail.

For their trail knowledge: Sean Lawson, Director of the Naturalist Program at Mad River Glen, who finally showed me the difference between a spruce and a fir on our hike up Burnt Rock Mountain; Katie Stewart, District Ranger, White Mountain National Forest, and Tim Yurkiewicz, who helped me sort out where to go around Mount Cabot and the Kilkenny Range, not to mention much of the Presidentials; and Pete Antos-Ketcham, Education Coordinator and Facilities Manager at the Green Mountain Club for helping me narrow down the choices in Vermont.

For their companionship, my many friends who hiked with me during the summer of 2004: Peter Knights and his daughters Carly and Macken-zie; Eileen Shiffrin; Lisa Grose; Steve and Cindy Berlack and their kids, Ron and Carolyn; Karen Carter and her sons Jake and Cole; Steve and Alice Andrews and their son Ethan; Tara Martin; Rick Moulton; Deborah Hannam and her children, Max, Benjamin, and Grace; Win and Janne Piper and their sons Win and Duncan; Jonathan Kenkel; Sheldon Perry; Paul Bousquet; Edie Lodi, Marc Valance and his son Quinn; Kate Carter; Wendel Behrend; Belle MacDougall; Peggy Shinn; Liz Venesky and Miles Galin; Lucinda Bain; Eva Merriam; and Bunny Merrill. It would have been a lonely summer on the trail without your company! Without your insights and trail suggestions, this *Best Hikes with Dogs* would have merely been *Good Hikes with Dogs*. Thank you for sharing your favorite routes with me. And mostly, the following dogs who hiked with me, slobbered on me, and let me give them an occasional biscuit or scratch behind the ears: Bravo, Bella, Casper, Cleo, Fudge, Hank, Jane, Kylee, Leo, Lil, Lucy (both of them), Max, Oliver, Patriot, Spam, and Zoya. Your pictures adorn these pages. Ruff!

PREFACE

As any author will confess, writing a book is a labor of love. In this case, it arises also from a love of hiking shared by both me and my dog. When Bravo sees my hiking boots or my day pack, his enthusiasm nearly bowls me over, figuratively and literally. He races to the door, sometimes between my legs or even over my head (if I am tying my bootlaces). He plants himself at the back of my car until I open the hatchback, then jumps aboard. He sits patiently all day back there until we set off, happy with the knowledge that he is "in"—he is going! It is usually a short wait, no more than a half hour for me to pack our gear and a lunch. Once in the car, he rides quietly for a couple of hours. But as soon as the pavement gets rougher and the car slows, a low whimper issues from the back. Within minutes, Bravo stands, excitement radiating off him like a sunburst, warming my heart. Some days I have to hike simply because of Bravo.

I have hiked in Vermont and New Hampshire for thirty years. Much of that mileage was with friends or alone. When I married my husband seventeen years ago, a dog was part of the deal. I have been fond of every dog we have owned, but Bravo is special. He is a true hiker-dog.

As I tired of the same old routes, I looked for information on more good hikes with dogs. I have a passion for the highest mountains, but they are often the most difficult to climb, with fixed ropes, ladders, boulder fields, and other dog deterrents. I was frustrated by the lack of detail in hiking guidebooks about these concerns, so rather than risk aborting a hike, I stayed with the same dozen or so trails.

During the winter of 2003, I was invited on a backcountry ski trip near Steamboat Springs, Colorado, to test new gear and apparel from Mountain Hardwear. Another writer, Dan Nelson, was on the trip. We agreed to swap books. I sent him my first book, *Ski Faster* (McGraw-Hill, 1999), and he sent me *Best Hikes with Dogs: Western Washington* (The Mountaineers Books, 2002). I was inspired. This book is the result.

I live on the border of Vermont and New Hampshire, within two hours of most hikes in either state. To write this book, I hiked over 300 miles and 100,000 vertical feet during the summer of 2004, mostly with Bravo, but also with a number of other dogs. I discovered countless dog-friendly hikes and dog-lovers, but most of all, I had the daily joy of walking

Bravo gives Jason a doggie kiss on the summit of Mount Hight.

through the woods with my favorite brown canine. If you ever want to feel absolute unconditional love, sit on the summit of a towering peak, hugging your dog. It is the pinnacle of warmth and affection. This book tells you how to get there.

PART 1

Hiking with Your Dog

With eye uprais'd, his master's looks to scan,
The joy, the solace, and the aid of man;
The rich man's guardian, and the poor man's friend,
The only being faithful to the end.

—George Crabbe, from "The Borough"
Source: *Dog Days, a Photographic Celebration
from the Hulton Getty Picture Collection*
(Harper-Collins, 2000)

Getting Ready
Should Your Dog Go Hiking?

The short answer is yes, but the real answer depends on your dog. Most dogs that are bigger than a kitten and smaller than a pony make excellent hiking companions—if they are physically fit for the level of hiking that you plan to do, if they are obedient, if they are socialized among both people and other dogs, and if the weather is not too hot. These are important ifs.

Hiking is more strenuous than walking. The terrain is uneven and usually involves vertical gain. If you spend more time watching television than exercising, chances are your dog does too. Certainly, if you anticipate a trail to be strenuous, then your dog will likely find it strenuous. Before committing your dog to a hike, make an honest assessment of his fitness level and be sure he is up to the expedition. If you plan to do a 10-mile hike, but your normal daily walks are only 2 miles, then a training program is in order.

Consider any health issues your dog may have. If he has a condition

Lil on the upper ledges of Mount Hunger

that might make hiking painful, such as hip dysplasia, a veterinarian might be able to prescribe medication that will ease his discomfort. Pregnant or nursing (lactating) dogs should wait until their "condition" has passed.

If you feel your dog is fit enough, then ask yourself whether he is well-behaved enough. Hiking may take place in wilderness areas, but that does not mean you will be by yourself. In fact, the odds are high that you will encounter other people and dogs on most trails in Vermont and New Hampshire. Before you take your dog into the backcountry, be sure he can heel, sit, stay, and come, preferably to your verbal command, although a whistle command is okay. Your dog should also be comfortable on a leash and, if off leash, be more interested in staying with you than chasing squirrels.

Just as important, your dog should be completely socialized among other dogs and humans. The trails in Vermont and New Hampshire are often narrow, with dense undergrowth on either side. You will be close to others when you pass on the trail or pause at the top of a popular mountain. If your dog is aggressive or overly protective, it is best to find another outdoor activity that is better suited to his personality. Likewise, if your dog is overly lovey-dovey, consider another dog-friendly sport (or more accurately another "friendly dog sport"), or at least select an unpopulated route. An extremely affectionate dog will hinder your pace and can be annoying to other hikers who do not like dogs.

Your canine should also miss the hike if he is prone to barking. Your dog may be an extroverted sap, but if he is a loud sap, you will be the least popular hiker on the trail. And any designated campsite that is regularly monitored by a ranger or staffed by a caretaker may ask you to leave if your dog barks too much.

Size matters, too. Like overweight people, overweight dogs are at a disadvantage on the trail. They have to work harder and put their bodies under more stress to cover the same ground, especially on steeper terrain. If you cannot feel your dog's ribs through his fur, then your pet is on the chubby side. He will be much happier in the backcountry if you put him on a diet and an exercise regimen before you go.

Size also refers to breed. There is a reason why most dogs on the trails in this region are fairly large breeds, particularly on longer, more difficult hikes. Labrador retrievers are the most common trail dog, but almost any breed or mixed breed over forty pounds should be able to handle any hike in this book—which is not to say that small dogs cannot trot down the trail as well as large ones can. A hyper Yorkshire terrier can humble a lazy black Lab if the trail is relatively smooth and short. However, small dogs have to take a lot more steps to cover the same territory, and they cannot stretch as far up or down a rock, so they may need a lift where a larger dog would not. There are definitely some trails that any dog can handle, and likewise, others that only the most exceptional mountain dog should attempt. For everything in between, it is a judgment call whether the breed is appropriate for the hike.

Age is actually more of a factor than breed. Like humans, as dogs age, their ability to handle the rigors of hiking lessens. Old dogs, like old people, have stiffer joints, arthritis, and other ailments that reduce their physical abilities. While smaller breeds tend to live longer than larger breeds, any dog age ten or older should be carefully assessed before bringing him on all but the easiest routes. Take it easy with puppies, too. Lack of obedience training aside, hiking up and down steep, uneven trails can adversely affect the development of a growing puppy's hips, shoulders, and other joints, which are not fully formed until they are at least nine months old in smaller breeds, and a year old in larger breeds.

Regardless of breed, if the weather is hot and humid, pick an easy, shaded hike to a pond, rather than an epic 4000-footer with 5 miles of trail above tree line. On the stickiest days, forget the hike and opt just for a pond, even if your pet is a model mountain dog. I call it the "85 Rule": If the day is above 85 degrees and above 85 percent humidity, a dog-friendly dock is much healthier for both you and your dog than even a moderate hike.

Assuming agreeable weather, in the end, deciding whether a dog is appropriate for a hike boils down to matching the difficulty of the hike with the ability of the dog. If you keep this in mind, you and your pet will have many enjoyable days together on the trail.

Fit for the Trail

Hiking is mainly an endurance sport, although it also requires leg power when the trail gets steep and balance when crossing a single log bridge. While your dog might forgo the bridge and opt to wade through the mud, he still needs the same lung and leg power you do.

Before the first hike of the year, take your dog for regular walks, preferably on trails or dirt roads in your area, but any type of walk is better than nothing. Gradually increase your mileage until your dog can handle a distance at least 25 percent greater than what you plan to hike without soreness or undue fatigue.

In addition to improving your dog's stamina, some diligent walking prior to your first hike will help toughen her pads. This is also a good time to get her used to wearing a harness and doggie "saddle bags" if you plan to have her carry her own supplies.

Have your veterinarian give your dog a complete physical before you go, to get a professional opinion on whether she is up for the outing. At the same time, have her toenails trimmed if they need it. A seasoned hiking dog's claws tend to stay short because they are constantly worn on the trail. The longer your dog's nails are, the more likely they are to split or tear on rugged terrain.

Check that your dog's shots, particularly for rabies, are up to date. There are rabid animals in the woods, but the more immediate risk is that you and your dog will not be allowed in a state forest or park area without an up-to-date rabies tag.

The other two common canine risks that are easy to prevent are Lyme disease and heartworm. Lyme disease is transmitted by deer ticks (the little black ones, not the big brown wood ticks). You greatly reduce your dog's chances of getting the disease if you administer a tick deterrent, like Frontline.

Heartworm is transmitted by mosquitoes. Dogs are at risk from early May through winter freeze-up. After testing negative for heartworm, monthly preventative heartworm pills are available through your veterinarian.

If you have a new puppy that you plan to take hiking, you might consider having its dew claws removed. (This is the odd claw that hangs uselessly at the back of the dog's ankle.) Tearing a dew claw is one of the most common injuries among canines in the wilderness. This is a simple procedure done by a veterinarian when puppies are young, especially to "backcountry dogs" such as those trained for hunting or dogsledding, which are susceptible to tearing a dew claw.

The first time you take your dog for a hike, keep it short, and be strict with trail protocol. Dogs are creatures of habit. If you insist on good trail etiquette from the start, they will quickly learn how to behave in the mountains and ultimately become stellar hiking companions.

Dog-mas

Federal and state agencies and trail maintenance organizations have rules for dogs in certain backcountry areas. For example, dogs are not allowed on hiking trails in national parks. This is not an issue in Vermont or New Hampshire because there are no national parks in either state, with the

The Appalachian Trail joins the Crawford Path, the oldest continually maintained hiking trail in the United States, as it approaches Mount Washington.

exception of the Appalachian Trail and the area around Mount Tom in Woodstock, Vermont. The forest around Mount Tom has the designation "National Historical Park," which is slightly different; in addition, Mount Tom itself is owned by the Town of Woodstock. Dogs are common on the entire trail system there.

The Appalachian Trail (AT) is considered the nation's skinniest national park. It extends from Georgia to Maine, passing through both Vermont and New Hampshire. In the southern half of Vermont, the AT coincides with the Long Trail (LT). The AT splits from the LT in Mendon, Vermont, where it turns east, crossing into New Hampshire in Hanover.

The LT goes the entire length of Vermont along the spine of the Green Mountains. The Green Mountain Club maintains the entire LT, and thus the portion of the AT that coincides with it. The Appalachian Mountain Club (AMC) oversees the AT in New Hampshire, although the Dartmouth Outing Club maintains the 50-mile section from Hanover to Mount Moosilauke.

Most areas of the AT in Vermont and New Hampshire are dog-friendly, although dogs must often be on a leash. For example, in Vermont, dogs must be leashed in alpine zones above tree line. Pets are not allowed in AMC huts in the White Mountains and should be leashed when hiking past a hut. It is worth checking with the local trail club for dog policy on a particular section of the AT/LT, particularly if the route is not listed in this book.

There are two national forests in this region, the Green Mountain National Forest in Vermont and the White Mountain National Forest in New Hampshire. Numerous state forests and parks lie within the national forests, each with specific rules concerning dogs. In general, expect leash areas to be in effect at trailheads, in campsites, and on summit areas. The specific pet policies, if any, for the routes in this book are noted at the beginning of each hike description.

Here are some of the general rules of the trail, for both dogs and humans:

In the national forests, controlled by the United States Forest Service (USFS), your dog must be on a leash in developed campsites. This is difficult to define exactly, but if the campsite is on the map, consider it a leash area. Camping is not allowed above tree line, which is defined as trees shorter than eight feet. Dogs should always be on a leash on the summit of a mountain, around campsites, or if you meet a ranger on the trail. It is also recommended that you keep your dog on a leash in all parking lots and near all trailheads. Owners are required to clean up after their pets.

In state parks and recreation areas, the rules vary according to the type of area. Pets are prohibited at most state beaches, picnic areas, and historic sites. Some state parks allow pets and others do not. In areas where pets are allowed, they must be leashed and attended at all times. You must clean up after your pet. You, as your dog's owner, are responsible for his actions. If another visitor to the state park complains about your dog's behavior, you will have to remove him from the park, which usually means the end of your outing, as pets should not be left alone in a vehicle, camper, carrier, or other type of enclosure at any time.

State forests tend to be more lenient with their dog rules. Be courteous and use common sense in these areas in order to maintain this privilege.

Dogs are not allowed on the hiking trails on Mount Monadnock near Jaffrey, New Hampshire. Mount Monadnock is reputed to be the most hiked mountain in the country, with over 50,000 visitors each year. Given the high number of people and the vertical cliffs on its upper trails, it is not a particularly dog-friendly peak anyway.

Finally, in more popular state parks, where rangers are on duty full-time at the gate to collect parking fees and oversee campsites, you may have to show your dog's proof of rabies vaccination. Usually a current rabies tag will suffice.

Leave No Trace

Dog owners must work doubly hard to limit their impact on the environment because there are two of you on the trail—you and your pet. Everyone who goes into the backcountry should practice Leave No Trace hiking and camping. The Leave No Trace Center for Outdoor Ethics, the national nonprofit organization that manages the Leave No Trace educational program, is dedicated to teaching people how to enjoy natural areas responsibly so that they remain beautiful and peaceful. While it is impossible to have zero impact, there are many ways to minimize it.

Dealing with Waste

Carry out everything that you carry in. This includes items that are biodegradable, like apple cores and orange peels. While they might degrade over a period of time, this can take much longer than you think depending on where they fall. In the meantime, they are not much more than unsightly litter. Consider letting your dog carry the trash if he wears a doggie pack. It is the perfect cargo for a dog because it can be jostled without a worry.

Some purists carry literally everything out, including human and dog waste and the food remnants from dirty pots and dishes. If you find this too extreme, there is another option for dealing with waste—burying it.

View past North Moat across the Presidential Dry River Wilderness to Mount Washington

Dig a cathole, at least six to eight inches deep, using a portable garden trowel. Put the waste (including used toilet paper) in the hole, then cover it and disguise the spot. Be sure it is at least 200 feet or about 75 paces from water sources, trails, shelters, and campsites. (See "Ten Canons of Canine Trail Etiquette," page 26, for more on cleaning up after your pet.)

Some shelters have designated dish-washing areas to avoid attracting unexpected visitors during the night, namely bears, raccoons, or skunks. If not, use a small amount of biodegradable soap if absolutely necessary, strain out the food particles, and scatter the dishwater at least 200 feet from your campsite. (Note: In Vermont, the Green Mountain Club asks backpackers to refrain from using any soap. Instead, use boiling water to sterilize dishes and waterless hand sanitizer.) You should hang the leftover food particles with the rest of your trash in one bag and the food you have yet to eat in another bag from a sturdy tree at night. The bags should be at least twelve feet in the air and at least six feet from the tree trunk.

Tread Lightly

Take only pictures; leave only footprints. Picking a flower may seem harmless, but it could be an endangered species. While dogs do not pick flowers, they may dig them up. Do not allow your dog to disturb plants or wildlife.

Stay on the trail. Unless you are walking on rock, every footstep you and your dog take impacts the trail, adding to erosion and ultimately leading to a trail repair or even a trail relocation. You can do a few things to delay this labor-intensive and sometimes costly task, such as walking through mud puddles, rather than around them. Walking around mud holes may keep your boots drier and cleaner, but it widens the trail over time. Also

avoid taking shortcuts and cutting corners on switchbacks. It may save a few seconds here and there, but it increases erosion and leaves unsightly scars in the woods.

Above tree line, it is vital that you and your dog stay on the trail, walking on rock as much as possible. Rocks do not wear out. Soil and plants do. Soil becomes compacted, and it sticks to your hiking boots and your dog's paws. Some fragile alpine plants may endure the harshest mountaintop environment, but one step on them and they could be gone forever.

Camp with Care

Camp on durable surfaces. The same is true for choosing a campsite. Rock may not be comfortable to sleep on, but it is the most durable surface. After that, putting a tent on a spot that is already impacted, preferably an existing campsite or another durable surface such as sand, gravel, dry grasses, or even snow, at least will not add to

Diapensia, a rare flower found in the alpine zones above tree line (elevations of 4000 feet or higher) in New Hampshire and Vermont

the problem. If you must put your tent on live plant life, like grass, try to set up your tent as late as possible in the day and break it down soon after you wake up to limit the time the flora is compressed. It only takes someone camping or walking on vegetation three times before impact is visible. Most importantly, rather than alter a site to fit your camping needs, find a site that is already appropriate. It should be at least 200 feet, or about 75 adult paces, from the trail and water sources.

Limit campfires to designated fire pits in developed camping areas. The days of old-fashioned campfires, except in designated fire pits at developed campsites, are long gone. Campfires are a forest fire hazard, particularly if you do not know how to control a fire or put it out completely. Scavenging for wood, even dead fallen wood, has a severe impact on the forest. Your footsteps trample plants, and the wood you pick up deprives small animals, bugs, and bacteria—all critical to a forest ecosystem—of shelter and food. Today, portable camp stoves and candle lanterns have replaced campfires, and stargazing has replaced fire gazing.

Peace and Quiet

Be considerate of others. Voices and barking carry, particularly across bodies of water. Keep your dog quiet and under control, and try to be as unobtrusive as possible. That way, everyone will enjoy their time in the woods.

For more information, go to *www.lnt.org* and, as always, contact the local trail maintenance club for specific rules or guidelines in a particular area.

Hiker Responsibility Code

The Hiker Responsibility Code has nothing to do with dogs in the backcountry, but it has everything to do with your safety there—yours and your dog's. This short list of reminders will help ensure you are prepared on any hike:

Be self-reliant. Before you start out, learn about the terrain, the condition of the trail, the weather, and how to use your gear.

Know when to turn back. Weather can change unexpectedly in the mountains. A route may take longer than you expect. You or your dog may become fatigued. Some of the most experienced mountaineers have perished because they had a single-minded goal and refused to give it up. Always set a turn-around time and stick to it no matter what, and if conditions take a turn for the worse, head for home. The mountains are not going anywhere. You can try again another time.

Know how to rescue yourself. An injury, a wrong turn, or a bad storm can turn even the tamest outing into a life-threatening situation. Do not assume you will be rescued quickly. Stay up to date on basic first aid. Always carry a whistle, a topo map, a compass, extra food, water, and clothing. If you are lost and cannot find the trail, make a decision—either stay put and wait for help, or follow the nearest stream downhill. In Vermont and New Hampshire, most water sources lead to a road in less than 10 miles (although those 10 miles might be extremely arduous). Many people carry cell phones when they hike in case of an emergency, but a signal is not reliable in the mountains. Most importantly, stay calm, and stay warm and dry to prevent hypothermia, so that when the rescue team finally finds you, you will still be alive.

Stay together. If you are hiking in a group, always hike at the pace of the slowest person.

Tell someone your plans. Before you depart, tell a reliable person at home what route you are taking and when you expect to return. Then stick to the plan!

For more information on the Hiker Responsibility Code, check out *www.hikesafe.com.*

Ten Canons of Canine Trail Etiquette

It is a privilege, not a right, to be able to hike with your dog. Every time you step onto a trail with your dog, you are both ambassadors for everyone else who hikes with dogs. With increasing numbers of people, and therefore dogs, on the trail systems in New Hampshire and Vermont, dog access has become a hot topic among many trail maintenance organizations and the state and federal agencies that control the majority of hiking trails here. While most dogs hike without problems, it only takes a few trailside incidents, a couple of outspoken dog-haters, or several expensive dog rescues for wilderness areas to become more restrictive to dogs. For this reason, it is critical that you take to heart the following "Ten Canons of Canine Trail Etiquette":

1. **Keep the dog-to-human ratio at 1:1.** If dogs outnumber people, it can be difficult to quickly control your dogs. That means putting a leash on them if they get on an animal scent or if other hikers and dogs approach. Plus, it is awkward to hike with only one dog on a leash when the trail is steep, narrow, eroded, or wet, all common conditions on New England trails. Trying to control two or more dogs, even well-behaved

dogs, is nearly impossible and could raise the chance of injury to a dog, yourself, or others.

2. **Limit the total number of dogs in your hiking group to two, regardless of the number of humans.** Three or more dogs hiking together become a pack of dogs, which can be intimidating to other hikers, particularly those uncomfortable around dogs. What is more, a group of dogs is less likely to mind their masters with that much peer pressure. A big group also increases the impact to the trail and the surrounding environment. Whenever there is a concentration of man and beast, the trample effect increases because paws and feet tend to land on the same spot. Dogs, like humans, usually follow each other closely. Let's say you plan a hike with four adults, four children, and two dogs—a group of ten. That is twenty-four feet heading up the trail together! Try to keep your total head count under ten.

3. **Put your dog on a leash whenever you meet others— people or dogs—on the trail.** Whether or not you are in a leash area, it is a courtesy to fellow hikers to put your dog on a leash whenever you are close to each other. You never know if the other person is fond of dogs or dog-phobic. It can be disconcerting for even the most avid dog-lover to see a loose dog come bounding down the trail at him, especially a large dog. And if there are children in the other party, a friendly dog could accidentally knock over a kid with an overly enthusiastic greeting, particularly if the dog surprises the approaching child, who may be tired and concentrating more on his next cookie than others on the trail.

Your dog may be friendly in general, but you never know what might set her off when she meets a stranger in the backcountry. An odd body odor, the sound of hiking poles clattering on the rocks, or a huge frame pack that makes the approaching person appear like a giant can put a dog on the defensive. In addition, dogs exhibit pack behavior. It is their nature to establish dominance or subservience when they meet other dogs. Even if Rover is a total beta dog, if he is on a leash you have better control over unexpected reactions, and you put the approaching hiker at ease.

In a perfect world, an approaching dog would be on a leash

Dogs should be on leashes around AMC huts, such as Greenleaf Hut on Mount Lafayette.

already, but if his master is not as dog-savvy as you are and you encounter a loose dog on the trail, you should still put your dog on a leash. You never know whether the strange dog will be aggressive or passive around your pet, but you can control the situation better if at least your dog is on a leash. Allow the two dogs to meet and sniff each other with an attitude of control. If you exude fear, your dog will sense it and become defensive. Speak in a friendly manner to both dogs, which sends the message that this is a friendly situation. As soon as the brief introduction is over, continue briskly on your way, ignoring the other dog.

Watch your dog. Dogs often pick up the scent of others on the trail before you see or hear them. If your pet pauses and suddenly becomes more alert, put him on a leash until the other people and dogs are out of sight.

4. **Dog-less hikers have the right-of-way.** The accepted rule of the trail is that uphill hikers have the right-of-way, but if you meet a dog-less human, he has the right-of-way no matter which way he is heading. Besides putting your dog on a leash, you and your dog should step aside. Command your dog to sit as the other hikers pass. This prevents you and your dog from accidentally bumping the other people. It also signals that you are in complete control of your pet.

As soon as you see an approaching party, find a wider spot that allows you to stop with your dog. Otherwise, if possible, step carefully to the uphill side of the trail, preferably onto a flat rock. Stepping uphill and onto a durable surface has less impact, and over time helps lessen erosion.

5. **No jumping up, sniffing, licking, growling, or barking.** The first three—jumping up, sniffing, and licking—should not be an issue if your dog is well trained and on a leash. If your dog growls or barks, a verbal "no" or "quiet" should be enough to keep the peace. If the problem is chronic, you might consider an electronic bark collar or specific obedience training. Regardless, delay taking your dog on the trail until he breaks the habit.

Sometimes the sniffing issue is limited to mountaintops and other destinations where you are most likely to be around other people and picnics. Dogs sniff as a way to identify other things and because they are natural hunters and scavengers. It is a rare dog that will not "ask" for a taste of someone else's lunch, but if you satisfy your dog with his own snacks and water, he will be less likely to beg from others.

6. **Shout a friendly hello to tell your dog that a friend, not a foe, approaches.** People usually greet each other on the trail, but it is a prerequisite when you hike with a dog. Most dogs are naturally protective of their masters. As soon as you see another person, say hello and exude friendliness. This tells your dog that the approaching person is not a threat and puts him at ease.

7. **Clean up after your dog—that includes dog poop.** Dogs may be animals, but they are not wild animals. Their refuse is not part of nature. Even the most avid dog-lover does not appreciate dog poop on the trail or near a campsite. As with human waste, either bag it or bury it in a cathole. If you bury

it, it should be 200 feet from the trails and water sources, and at least six to eight inches deep. If you are camping along trails maintained by the Green Mountain Club (in Vermont), the club permits disposal of dog poop in human outhouses, but only the poop, not the bag you use to transport it. The club asks dog owners to pack the poop out if day-hiking.

8. **Obey the rules of the trail**, particularly if dogs are not allowed or should be leashed. This might sound obvious, but it is not always followed, which is the reason the Green Mountain Club stations "caretakers" on the summit of Mount Mansfield. These caretakers educate hikers about the natural history of the area and how to reduce their impact on the environment and on other hikers. The alpine vegetation is so rare and fragile that one pawprint could kill it forever. Technically, these trail ambassadors should not be needed, but they are. If you are in a leash area, abide by the rule to conserve the privilege of hiking there with dogs. And if an area does not allow dogs, do not go there with one.

In high alpine areas, such as the summit of Mount Mansfield, rare fragile sedges look like grass.

9. **Stay on the trail.** With the exceptions of setting up a camp-site, relieving oneself, cleaning pots, bathing, or letting another person pass on a narrow trail, always stay on the trail. That goes for your dog too. In fact, most dogs naturally stick to the trail because they want to be with their masters and the footing is easier. Of course, many dogs, particularly near the trailhead when they are full of energy and excitement, bound through the woods with reckless abandon. Some dogs never lose that enthusiasm, romping ten miles to your two, as they run ahead, circle around, sniff every stump, and chase butterflies. The party line is certainly to keep your dog with you and under control at all times, but let's be reasonable. Use your judgment. Let your dog romp, but pick her moments when she won't bother other people, dogs, or wildlife, and where she will have limited impact on the environment. That said, your dog should always be in sight and within range of your commands.

10. **Leave plants and wild animals alone.** At the risk of being redundant, this is worth emphasizing. Certainly, the fragile plants atop the highest peaks should not be trampled or picked, but the same goes for the most common plants at lower elevations. If your dog nibbles a few dandelions, it will not hurt anything, but if it paws the plant or digs, it will. Common plants are necessary for controlling trail erosion.

Likewise, do not allow your pet to terrorize the native fauna. A dog rarely catches anything, but the chase forces a wild animal to expend extra energy, which might weaken it among its natural predators, particularly during the winter when food sources are scarce. It goes without saying that predatory animals should be given a wide berth. If your dog is aggressive toward a bear, the bear might simply run away, or it might attack in self-defense, to protect its young or in territorial defense—and you, not your dog, could be the victim.

Good Dog Sense

In addition to the rules of the trail that various government agencies, trail maintenance organizations, and conservation groups assert, there are several more things to keep in mind when hiking with your pet in New Hampshire and Vermont, for the health and safety of both you and your dog.

Fire Towers

A number of peaks in Vermont and New Hampshire have old fire towers on top, which are a big reason to climb them. The fire towers are fun to climb (if you are not afraid of heights) and transform a viewless summit into a breathtaking wonder. Most are open to the public. They are in various degrees of disrepair, but generally safe—for humans. They are not safe for dogs.

Fire towers are not solid structures but cabins on tall stilts. The stairs are steep, narrow, and without risers, winding upward inside permanent scaffolding with little more than a handrail for support and protection. The climb up the stairs, usually over fifty feet, is a dizzying, windy affair for humans. Dogs usually become downright disoriented. Small dogs threaten to fall through the wide spaces. Large dogs have trouble turning around.

Most canines cannot make it to the lookout cabin, and if they do, the space is extremely cramped inside for more than a couple of people, let alone a nervous dog. And all dogs stay in the middle of the steps, making it difficult for others to pass them without getting bowled over.

Fire towers are one of the pleasures of hiking in the Green Mountains and the White Mountains, but leave your dog at the bottom on a leash, with a friend, or tied securely to the base or a tree away from the steps, both for his safety and for yours.

Cliff Areas

Cliff areas are among the other more desirable destinations when hiking in New Hampshire and Vermont—for humans. Reaching a cliff may be the goal or a bonus along the way. In either case, it is a dangerous area for a dog. Not that dogs

Fire tower on Smarts Mountain purposely jump off cliffs—they do not—but they will sense your excitement (and trepidation if you are scared of heights) and get excited themselves, often bounding ahead as a natural reaction. Oops! Too far! You get the picture. There are rarely guard rails in the mountains. As you approach a cliff area, be sure to put your dog on a leash and keep him calm and close.

Ladders

Sometimes a trail crew will fix a ladder, usually made from two-by-fours nailed together, to a rock wall to help hikers, but it will not help dogs. Some ladders are short, only four to six rungs. In those cases, a dog can usually find another route up or down the rock, either next to the trees or on the rock itself. However, if you come to a tall ladder, consider turning back. It is dangerous to carry your pet up a tall ladder, especially a large, squirming pet. In this book, while several routes have short ladders, they are at shallow inclines (similar

The ladder on Mount Morgan, a doggie no-no

to steps), and in each case there is an easy way for your dog to continue without negotiating the ladder.

Water

While water is not a prerequisite for a good dog hike, it is likely your dog's favorite part of the day. Dogs need water to cool off on the outside and to stay hydrated on the inside. Some dogs will not pause at a stream crossing if you do not. Stop near trailside water longer than you might by yourself, to give your dog a chance to use it.

There is another consideration when it comes to water: whether to drink it. Parasites, such as *Giardia lamblia,* bacteria, and viruses have become

Hank takes a drink in a clear running stream.

common even in remote mountain streams. People are warned never to drink untreated water in the backcountry, no matter how clear and pure it looks. Chlorine and iodine are not effective at ridding water of parasites, but they do kill bacteria and viruses. The recommendation for humans is that *Giardia* and other microorganisms should be filtered or boiled out. But what about dogs?

Dogs are susceptible to waterborne illnesses too, so technically, you should discourage your dog from drinking water along the trail. Yeah, right. Only the most prudish dogs will ignore a babbling brook, and most will jump into a swampy pool of stagnant algae if they are hot and thirsty enough. While the party line says no, the voice of reason says guide your dogs to clear, running water as much as you can. In the rare case that your pet contracts diarrhea or shows other symptoms, take him to a veterinarian as soon as possible.

Above all, always carry water and a water dish (the soft, collapsible type take up zero space and weigh next to nothing) for your dog. Never count on water along any trail in New Hampshire or Vermont. Streams frequently dry up, and dogs are not allowed around water sources for shelters and campsites.

Feeding Your Dog

Recently, a number of doggie energy bars have been introduced, but they are not created equally. Dogs, like people, burn muscle glycogen when they exercise, which must be replenished, particularly on an overnight or multi-day trip. The trick is to give your dog a quick nibble (not a meal) about every forty-five minutes to one hour of steady hiking, then again within a half hour after the end of the hike. This snack at the end of the hike is the most critical, because immediately after exertion, a dog receives glycogen directly into her muscles from her digestive tract, without having to process the glycogen through her liver.

When it comes to the main meal, a working dog should get only one meal a day, preferably at the end of the day. For maximum recovery after a day on the trail, feed your pooch his normal meal about two hours after hiking.

Look for products that are high in protein, fat, and maltodextrose, a carbohydrate that dogs digest quickly without a huge insulin spike. Active dogs have different nutritional needs than active humans, especially when it comes to fat. Fat is not bad for dogs. Except for miniature schnauzers, dogs do not get coronary disease. In addition, dogs have a 30 percent greater capacity to metabolize oxygen than humans do. That means it is much harder for dogs to become anaerobic (when you feel short of breath and your legs feel like lead due to lactic acid buildup), so they are better able to use fat as energy. Dogs are omnivorous, but they did not evolve with carbos as a major part of their diet.

Grooming

A hiking dog needs lots of attention beyond the scratch-behind-the-ear variety. Depending on their coats, dog fur is a magnet for mud, burrs, leaves, and small seeds. On some long-haired breeds, if their fur gets knotted enough, they will refuse to move another inch. Be diligent about keeping your dog's coat clean and detangled.

The Essentials
Gear for You

There is an old saying: "Don't like the weather in the mountains? Wait a minute." New England weather, particularly in the backcountry, can turn from sunny to stormy without notice. For this reason, it is crucial that you bring the right gear, even if your outing seems short and tame.

New Hampshire and Vermont trails are always muddy and often require stream crossings without bridges. Take care of your feet with waterproof-breathable hiking boots, preferably those with sturdy Vibram soles, which give you support and lessen fatigue from walking on rocks and uneven surfaces.

Foot-care also includes wearing technical wool socks. These aren't your father's rag wool socks. A hiking-specific pair of technical wool socks will wick moisture from your feet, give you support around the arch area, and cushion from below. On the summit of a long, rugged mountain, it helps to put on fresh socks, or at least switch the tired ones to the opposite feet for the hike down.

Raingear is also critical, preferably waterproof-breathable pants and a jacket. These will protect you from precipitation and wind. Always carry raingear, even on the hottest summer day. A fleece pullover or a soft-shell jacket provides a layer of insulation (and wind protection depending on the fabric). The temperature drops at least 3 degrees for every thousand feet of vertical gain, and that does not include wind-chill. Fleece remains warm when wet and dries quickly.

There is another saying in the mountains: "Cotton kills." Cotton absorbs moisture, but holds it against your body, which can lead to hypothermia. Instead of a cotton T-shirt, wear a shirt (base layer) made of a fabric that wicks moisture away from your skin and dries super-fast.

You should carry two hats, a warm one made of wool or fleece and a nylon ball cap or wide-brimmed one. You lose over 50 percent of your body heat through your head. If the temperature drops, the best way to check the chill is to put on a warm hat. The nylon ball cap has nothing to do with warmth, but you will likely wear it 90 percent of the time, even on hot days, because it provides protection from the sun and the bugs.

Northern New England is notorious for its blackflies and mosquitoes, particularly during the spring and early summer. The higher the DEET content in a bug repellent, the better it works and the longer it lasts. Most authorities recommend formulas with at least 30 percent DEET for real protection. Apply your bug spray over your sunscreen.

A light pair of fleece, Windstopper, or leather gloves takes the chill off human paws on cold days, especially when you have to hold a leash.

It is a good idea to pack a headlamp or flashlight. You never know when you might get stuck on the trail after dark. A headlamp is preferable. It allows you to hike hands-free, so you can handle a leash and still pet your dog at will or grab a hand-hold if you need it.

Bring along a whistle. If you get lost, you can sustain a call for help with a whistle hours longer than yelling.

If you go on an overnight trip, you should always bring a tent, even if you are planning to sleep in a shelter. Most backcountry shelters are available on a first-come, first-served basis, and they might be full when you arrive. Even if there is space, your shelter-mates might not appreciate a dog near their pillows. In general, day hikers do not carry emergency shelters in this region because tree line is never far and a shelter is rarely more than a few miles away, particularly if you are hiking along the AT or LT.

One other helpful item is a bandanna or similar all-purpose rag. Some might argue that this is the most useful item in your pack. It is a sweatband, handkerchief, first-aid item, napkin, washcloth, and a strap all in one.

Here is a list of items that should always be in your pack. This is not a complete list of everything you need for a week in the woods. It is a checklist of the basics you should bring *every time* you go hiking in New Hampshire and Vermont.

The Ten Essentials: A Systems Approach

1. Navigation (map and compass)
2. Sun protection (sunscreen, sunglasses)
3. Insulation (extra clothing including rain gear)
4. Illumination (headlight or flashlight)
5. First-aid supplies
6. Fire (fire starter and matches or lighter)
7. Repair kit and tools (including knife)
8. Nutrition (extra food)
9. Hydration (extra water)
10. Emergency shelter (if you don't carry it, know where to find it)

Gear for Your Dog

Those are your essentials. You should also have the ten canine essentials
for your dog:

The Ten Canine Essentials

1. **Obedience training.** Before you set foot on a trail, make sure your
   dog is trained and can be trusted to behave when faced with other
   hikers, other dogs, wildlife, and an assortment of strange scents and
   sights in the backcountry.
2. **Doggie backpack.** This lets the dog carry his own gear.
3. **Basic first-aid kit** (details listed on page 44).
4. **Dog food and trail treats.** You should bring more food than your
   dog normally consumes since she will be burning more calories than
   normal, and if you end up spending an extra night in the woods, you
   need to feed the pup, too.
5. **Water and water bowl.** Do not count on water along the trail
   for the dog. Pack enough extra water to meet all of your dog's drinking needs. Use the same bowl for dog food to conserve weight.
6. **Leash and collar or harness.** Even if your dog is absolutely trained
   to voice command and stays at heel without a leash, sometimes leashes
   are required by law or as a common courtesy, so you should have one
   handy at all times.
7. **Insect repellent.** Like some people, some animals have a strong negative reaction to DEET-based repellents. Before leaving home, dab a
   little repellent on a patch of your dog's fur to see if she reacts to it. Look
   for signs of drowsiness, lethargy, and/or nausea. Restrict applications
   to those places that a dog cannot lick, such as the back of the neck and
   around the ears (staying well clear of the eyes and inner ears), where
   mosquitoes will be looking for exposed skin to bite.
8. **ID tags and picture identification.** Your dog should always
   wear an ID tag. Consider microchipping as well. To do this, a vet
   injects a tiny encoded microchip under the skin between your dog's
   shoulders. If your dog becomes lost and is picked up by the authorities or is taken to a vet's office, a quick pass over the dog's back
   with a hand scanner will allow the shelter or hospital staff to identify
   your dog and notify you. Most vets and shelters automatically scan
   unknown dogs for microchips. The picture ID should go in your pack.

If your dog is lost, you can use the picture to quickly make flyers to post in surrounding communities.

9. **Dog booties.** These can be used to protect dog paws from rough ground or harsh vegetation. They are also great for keeping bandages secure if a dog injures a pad.

10. **Compact roll of plastic bags and a trowel.** Use the bags to clean up after your dog on popular trails. When conditions warrant, use the trowel to dig a cathole, deposit your dog's waste, and fill the hole.

Bravo carries his gear in his doggie backpack.

Canine First Aid
Common Dog Injuries and Afflictions

Dogs suffer many of the same injuries on the trail that people do, and a few that people do not. Dogs get sore muscles, sprains and strains, sore paws, and muscle cramps, just as their masters do. They can also tear a pad, a claw, or a dew claw. Getting your dog in good shape before you go hiking will go a long way toward preventing injuries. And even when a little sore, dogs are resilient and often retain their enthusiasm for an outing.

Major injuries are a different story and should be treated seriously. It is always a good idea to put a muzzle on a dog that is scared or in pain, even if she is normally gentle and friendly. The key on the trail is to watch your dog for any sign of distress, such as a limp, constant scratching at a certain area, or an abnormally slow pace. If your dog is not acting her usual self, stop walking and diagnose the cause. In the case of near drowning, major puncture wounds, broken bones, or other serious injuries, treat your dog for shock as you would a human by keeping her comfortably warm. Immobilize the traumatized area, while you wait for a litter to transport her to an animal hospital. A dog will respond to mouth-to-mouth resuscitation and CPR if her condition merits them.

Luckily, most dog injuries in the backcountry are minor:

Torn claw or dew claw. If your dog tears a dew claw, stop the bleeding by applying pressure. Then wrap the claw with gauze and tape. Be careful the wrap is not so tight that it restricts blood flow to the paw. A bad toenail split should get the same bandage treatment, but first apply a bit of styptic powder to speed up blood clotting. After bandaging a torn toenail, you should make sure your dog wears a bootie to prevent further injury and to keep the area clean.

Cut pad. To treat a cut pad, apply a bit of antiseptic to the wound, then wrap it with gauze and tape. Be careful not to tape the paw too tightly; it should still have normal articulation. After bandaging the paw, have your dog wear a bootie to prevent further injury and to keep the area clean.

Muscle sprains or soreness. Dogs usually respond well to dog-specific anti-inflammatories and pain relievers. Do not give your dog ibuprofen (Motrin, Advil) or Tylenol, as these can cause serious harm. If your dog continues to limp, he may have a more serious injury, such as a torn ACL (anterior cruciate ligament), and a visit to the veterinarian is in order.

Insect bites. A dab of calamine lotion will take the itch out of a dog's bug bites if you can get through the fur to the skin. If your pet is stung by a bee, look for the stinger and pull it out with tweezers if you can.

Ticks. Check your dog for ticks at least once per day. If a wood tick is biting your dog, it will blow up like a miniature balloon. To remove the tick, use tweezers to pinch the area where the tick's head enters the skin. Squeeze firmly and lift until the dog's skin rises slightly, then wait a moment until the tick withdraws under the pressure of being pulled. A bit of skin may come off with the tick, but that is okay. The important thing is to get the whole tick and not leave the head behind. Rub a little antiseptic ointment on the area. If your dog was bitten by a deer tick, watch the area around the bite carefully for several days to see if red rings appear, indicators of Lyme disease. If your dog later seems achy and sluggish, these could be symptoms of Lyme disease. Take your pet to a vet immediately for treatment with antibiotics.

Dehydration and overheating. Dogs have limited options when it comes to dispelling heat from their bodies. The primary method is panting. Soaking their groin area in mud or cool water is helpful, too. Some breeds handle heat better if you have their groin area shaved, but most simply pant. Interestingly, fur can help, insulating a dog from the heat. But as soon as a dog begins to work hard hiking, you should watch him carefully for overheating, which could lead to heat stroke.

Dehydration is the biggest contributor to overheating. Always carry water for your dog and give him healthy drinks every forty-five minutes to an hour. Between drinks, if he has foam around his mouth, it helps to wash it away with a squirt-top water bottle. The foam is not necessarily a sign that your dog is overheating, but it does inhibit his panting efficiency.

Do not worry about heavy panting, either. We tend to humanize our dogs. If we are out of breath during a steep uphill slog, then we assume that our dog's panting means he is out of breath too. Not necessarily.

Always carry water and a portable bowl for your dog.

Dogs have a much higher anaerobic threshold than humans. They are probably panting hard because their physical output is generating excess heat, and they need to vent it. However, if a dog starts to lag behind and his tongue is extended far to the side, he is likely overheating. Stop immediately and give him some water. If possible, find a stream or a mud puddle he can soak in. Allow your dog to fully recover before continuing. Slow your pace to prevent a relapse.

Skunk spray. There are many old wives' tales about how to remove skunk spray from a dog. Most do not work, and the one that does—a bath in tomato juice—is impractical. Unfortunately, a wet dog smells worse. There are several skunk odor remedies available through local pet stores or your vet. Your best bet is to shampoo your dog thoroughly. (Flex shampoo works well.) A hint of the odor might linger for a while, but at least the worst of it will be gone.

Porcupine quills. A face full of porcupine quills is a dog's—and dog owner's—worst nightmare. It is difficult to put a muzzle on the dog because of the quills, but it is nearly impossible to pull them out and keep your fingers. Most dogs will tolerate one or two yanks, but after that they will likely snap at you. For those one or two, grasp the quill with needlenose pliers where it enters the skin, then give a quick, assertive pull. Do what you can on the trail, but get your dog to a vet as soon as possible, where the bulk of the quills can be removed while the dog is sedated.

Animal bites. Jagged open wounds caused by other dogs or wild animals should be washed with potable water. Cover the wound with gauze and tape, and apply pressure to stop bleeding if necessary. Take your dog to a vet as soon as possible.

Burns. Dogs are most likely to get burned in the backcountry if they get too close to a camp stove and knock a pot of boiling water over. Whatever the cause of the burn, soak the area in cold water, if available, to cool it off. Apply antiseptic, then lightly bandage the burn to keep it clean. Visit a vet as soon as possible if your dog's skin blisters or looks charred.

Poisoning. Most dogs love to roll around on dead fish, which only serves to make them smell bad. But if they eat any of it, they could get extremely sick. The same goes for that two-pound chocolate bar that was supposed to fuel the humans in your group for a long weekend in the woods. Whatever the source, if your dog eats something poisonous, immediately induce vomiting, then get her to a vet as soon as possible.

Poisonous plants. Of the three rash-inducing poisonous plants found in the United States—poison ivy, poison oak, and poison sumac—only poison ivy and poison sumac exist in Vermont and New Hamsphire. Poison sumac is rare, found only on the edges of wetlands. Poison ivy is ubiquitous. It grows at most locations below 2000 feet, particularly in the central and southern parts of both states where the winters are less harsh.

Poison ivy is particularly fond of the edges of trails where it gets sunlight but will not get trampled. While poison ivy is most commonly a ground cover that can be anywhere from a couple inches to a couple feet high, it is actually a vine that turns woody as it climbs a host tree. Old poison ivy vines can be four inches or more in diameter. The saying, "Leaves of three, let it

Poison Ivy

be," is advice worth taking. Poison ivy, in its ground cover form, has obvious clusters of three leaves. In the spring, the stems and leaves have a reddish tint, which also helps to identify it.

The poison in poison ivy is urushiol, an oil. It is throughout the plant and can persist more than five years after the plant dies. While dogs rarely have a reaction to poison ivy, they can give it to their masters. If Fido wades through a patch of the stuff and you rub his belly, the oil will be on your hands. If you rub your chin, then you will get an itchy, bumpy rash on your chin. If Fido sits in your lap while you are wearing shorts, your thighs will get it too, unless you wash it off. You have a two-hour window to remove the oil, which can be done with soap and water. The only way to know if you have washed yourself in time and if you were thorough enough is to wait. It can take up to a week for the rash to appear, and then another week to dry up. Do not worry about spreading the rash to others. Assuming you have taken a shower since your hike, the oil is long gone.

What Goes in a Doggie First-aid Kit?

Bringing a first-aid kit for your dog is essential on any hike. A comprehensive canine first-aid kit includes the following items:

Instruments

- Scissors/bandage scissors/toenail clippers/tweezers
- Rectal thermometer (a healthy dog should show a temperature of 101 degrees)

Cleansers and Disinfectants

- Hydrogen peroxide, 3 percent
- Betadine
- Canine eyewash (available at large pet supply stores)

Topical Antibiotics and Ointments (non-prescription)

- Calamine lotion
- Triple antibiotic ointment (Bacitracin, Neomycin, or Polymyxin)
- Vaseline
- Stop-bleeding powder

Medications

- Enteric-coated aspirin or Bufferin
- Imodium-AD
- Pepto-Bismol

Dressings and Bandages

- Gauze pads (4 inches square) or gauze roll
- Non-stick pads
- Adhesive tape (one- and two-inch rolls)

Miscellaneous

- Muzzle
- Dog booties
- Any prescription medication your dog needs

For Extended Trips

Consult your vet about other prescription medications that may be needed in emergency situations, including:

- Oral antibiotics
- Eye/Ear medications
- Emetics (to induce vomiting)
- Pain-relief medications and anti-inflammatories
- Suturing materials for large open wounds

Wildlife Encounters

If you are observant, the signs of wildlife are everywhere in the woods. Tracks in the mud, fur caught in bark, and claw marks are just a few of the clues to the types of animals in the woods around you. While the evidence is obvious, it is a rare occasion that you will actually see anything bigger than a squirrel or a grouse.

Most wildlife is nocturnal and extremely shy. The most common encounters are in campsites, when people do not hang their food properly or when they leave food traces or other scented items on the ground or in their tents. It is important to keep your dog in your tent at night so she cannot chase critters in the woods or provoke a hungry bear that wanders by. Your dog will likely smell it and might get agitated. Hold your dog firmly and try to keep her calm until the animal outside your tent has departed.

Rabies

Any animal can get rabies, but raccoons, skunks, bats, and foxes are among the more common carriers of this deadly disease. If a wild animal approaches, particularly during daylight hours and particularly if its fur is mangy and it drools or has foam around its mouth, put your dog on a leash immediately, grab a long sturdy stick if possible, then immediately depart the area. Keep a constant eye on the animal, which is likely rabid. Rabies is transmitted through saliva and spinal fluid. If the animal continues to approach, use the stick to keep it at a distance from you and your dog. If you or your dog is bitten and it breaks the skin, even if your dog has a current rabies shot, seek medical attention immediately. If you or your dog touches the animal in any way, you must wash the area thoroughly with soap and water. The rule of thumb is to scrub for twenty minutes. Notify a game warden as soon as possible to report the animal.

Bears

The black bear is the only species of bear in the Northeast, found mainly in wilder wooded areas. There are collared immature bears in the area around Smarts Mountain and Mount Cube in New Hampshire, which are being introduced into the wild after being orphaned as cubs. But even these bears are shy around humans. In general, a black bear will avoid hikers, but a hungry one will raid a campsite if it smells food, and its sense of smell is very keen. A bear can smell food even in zip-lock bags. It will also defend a natural food source and its young. As with all animals, your dog will likely sense the bear before you do. When dogs pick up bear scent or the scent of any large animal, most will pause decisively and begin to growl nervously, although a few breeds (hounds in particular) will want to chase it. Put your dog on a leash right away! A loose dog might provoke a bear enough to attack. To escape, the dog may run behind you for protection, and guess who gets mauled.

To minimize the chance of a bear encounter, do the following:

- Keep your dog on a leash or in your tent when you are sleeping.
- Hike in a group during daylight.
- Make noise, talking or singing as you walk.
- Leave hair spray, cologne, scented soaps, and scented hand lotions at home.
- Never eat food or feed your dog in your tent.
- Do not clean fish within 100 feet of your campsite.
- Always hang food, trash, and other scented items in designated bear bags away from your shelter or campsite.

If you find yourself close to a bear, here are some guidelines:

- Remain calm and keep a firm grip on your dog's leash at heeling length. Do not run, as this might trigger a prey-chase reaction. You cannot outrun a bear, which can sprint at speeds up to 35 miles per hour, and it can climb a tree much more efficiently than you can.
- Talk calmly in a low voice, which tells the bear you are human.
- Hold your free arm out to the side, or open your jacket and hold it out to make yourself seem larger.
- Do not look the bear in the eye. Bears perceive eye contact as a threat or a challenge.
- Slowly move upwind of the bear if you can do so without crowding it. If the bear smells you as human, it might retreat.
- If the bear charges anyway, or even bluffs a charge (which is often a precursor to the real thing), let your dog go. Fight back by kicking or punching. If it perceives you as difficult prey, it might depart in search of an easier meal.

Catamounts (Mountain Lions)

Wild cats, such as lynx and bobcat, are rare indeed in New Hampshire and Vermont, but they do exist. Although cougars—also called mountain lions, catamounts, pumas, or panthers—have been officially nonexistent in this region for almost a century, recent sightings of "large wild cats" by veteran outdoorsmen and large feline footprints lead some biologists to think a few cougars may again roam here. An encounter with a cougar or any wild cat is unlikely, particularly if you hike with a large dog. Lynx and bobcat are small and will not hunt you, but a hungry catamount might go after a child or a small dog that strays too far from your group.

If you do meet a catamount on the trail, stay calm and do the following:

- Do not run. This will trigger the cat's prey-chase response.
- Look at the animal and appear aggressive. Always maintain eye contact, which is a show of dominance.
- Keep your dog on its leash and by your side. A cat is less likely to go after you if you are two against one.
- Try to back away slowly.
- If the cat attacks, try to remain standing and do not take your eyes off it. Fight back aggressively. Throw things at it, such as your camera, water bottles, and your pack, as long as you do not have to bend over to pick them up. Shout loudly. If the cat finds you difficult prey, it will likely retreat.

Skunks, Porcupines, Raccoons

These and other smaller critters that are not predatory can be real pests in the forests, particularly at night in your campsite. Stay in your tent with your dog. If your food is hanging correctly, they will likely wander off after awhile.

Moose

Moose are the most likely large animal that you will see in the woods, particularly in swampy areas. A veritable wall of animal, weighing up to 1800 pounds, they can move surprisingly fast when provoked, charging at 35 miles per hour. They often use hiking trails because the footing is easier. Like all wild animals they will usually wander away if humans are near, although sometimes they will just stand and stare, and in rare instances they will charge if protecting young (springtime) or during the rutting season (early fall). If a moose blocks the trail, keep your dog on his leash, then shout loudly to shoo the beast away. If the moose does not move, or if it seems aggressive—dropping its ears and looking agitated—take a detour yourself. And if it charges, your best chance is to put a large tree between you and the animal, then run if you get an opening. A moose will not pursue you very far. It is not a predator, and

Moose track in the mud on Moose Mountain

once the threat (you and your dog) is no longer perceived, it will likely amble away.

Weather

The single biggest danger to hikers and their dogs in New Hampshire and Vermont is the weather. Because the mountains here are low compared to places like the Rockies or the Sierra Nevadas, and because natural disasters like hurricanes, tornadoes, and earthquakes are rare, people might not take these mountains as seriously. Do not be fooled.

Lightning

If you are hiking and hear thunder, assume lightning too, even if you do not see it, because lightning causes thunder. Some of the best hikes in this region are on exposed ridges and bald summits, where the rock is typically loaded with iron. Just the fact that you are higher than the rock underfoot makes you susceptible to a lightning strike. At the slightest hint of a storm, head immediately below tree line to an area where the trees are at least twice as tall as you are. If this is impossible, try to find a low spot on the ridge where you can hunker down. Hold your dog closely. Even below tree line, it is not safe to use a tree for shelter, especially a tall tree. Find the lowest ground and crouch down (do not lie down) until the storm passes. If there are other people with you, spread out, so that if lightning strikes, it does not strike everyone in your party.

Wind

It is a rare day when the wind is not blowing on a mountaintop in New Hampshire and Vermont. The highest winds in the world have been

A weather warning at tree line on Mount Monroe

recorded on the top of Mount Washington. While it is usually not strong enough to knock you over, it will pull heat out of your body very quickly, especially if you are wet from either sweat or rain, causing hypothermia. Always carry wind-blocking garments and a wool hat when hiking. A jacket and pants made of a waterproof-breathable material can double as raingear. The trick to preventing hypothermia is staying warm and dry.

Humidity

High humidity is the norm in northern New England, particularly during the summer, which is prime hiking time. Humidity augments the effects of heat, and it saps your energy. The only defense against it for you and your dog is to stay hydrated. Bring a change of shirt to stay drier.

Snow, Sleet, Hail, Freezing Rain

It can snow on any mountain in New Hampshire or Vermont at any time of the year, so be prepared with layers of clothing, a hat, and gloves. If your dog is sensitive to cold weather, consider bringing a canine coat for her to wear on the summit.

Using This Book

A guidebook cannot provide all the details of a route, nor stay completely current. Trail conditions, stream crossings, access roads, government rules, even the routes themselves change over time. Before departing on any hike, check with the organization that maintains the trail for the latest information. A phone number and website are listed at the beginning of each hike description, along with any fees, permits, or pet policies if applicable.

In New England, a trail marking—typically a small vertical rectangle of paint on a tree or on immovable rock—is commonly called a "blaze." Technically, when you stand at one blaze, you should be able to see the next one, although that is often not the case. Paint wears off. Trees fall down. Trails get rerouted. But blazes are still an excellent guide in the woods. The Appalachian Trail (AT) and Long Trail (LT) always have white blazes. Trails that access the AT/LT have blue blazes. Other trails can be any color, but they are usually yellow or red. The blaze color for a particular trail is given the first time a trail name is mentioned in a trail description. When in doubt, call ahead to the contact club or agency to find out how a particular route is marked.

When hiking, if you see a double blaze (one blaze on top of another blaze of the same color), that means the trail is about to turn. If the trail is on bedrock, turns are usually shown by a blaze with a bend in the middle, and often with arrows at either end of it. Rock cairns—man-made piles of rock—also mark the route on most open slab and above tree line. If you cannot see a blaze and the trail is not obvious, look for the cairns, which can be particularly helpful if visibility diminishes.

A topographical (topo) map, an elevation profile, and the name of the coinciding USGS map are also included with each hike. Although they are still used by backcountry travelers, many USGS maps date back to the 1950s. The contours and natural landmarks are likely accurate, but the trails, campsites, and other manmade features, such as fire towers, might not be. The Appalachian Mountain Club (AMC) and the Green Mountain Club (GMC) are also excellent sources of up-to-date maps for the majority of hikes in this book. They provide the maps-of-choice for regular hikers in Vermont and New Hampshire.

Hikes within a particular region, such as "Vermont's Northeast Kingdom," are listed alphabetically by each destination's proper name. If you are traveling to a particular area of Vermont or New Hampshire and wish to find a dog-friendly hike there, check the main map in the front of the book for the hikes that are recommended there, then read about the hikes listed within that region.

The location of each trail and its trailhead are listed with the other information at the beginning of the hike. Distance, elevation gain, and hiking time are given for the entire hike, start to finish. Hiking time is merely a rough estimate, which assumes a moderate pace with periodic rest stops and a half hour at the summit or other scenic destination. The estimates are conservative, but a "moderate" pace for one person might seem extremely slow or fast to another. Use the hiking times in this book as a reference for planning your outing, not as a gauge of hiking prowess.

To determine whether a route is appropriate for you and your dog, pay close attention to its difficulty rating. Hikes in this book are rated 1 to 4 paws, which translates as follows:

> **1 paw = easy** (under 3 miles round trip and less than 500 feet vertical climb), appropriate for any dog, including older puppies and healthy senior dogs
> **2 paws = moderate** (3 to 5 miles round trip and/or 500 feet to 1500 feet vertical climb)
> **3 paws = ambitious** (5 to 7 miles round trip and/or 1500 feet to 2000 feet vertical climb)

4 paws = strenuous (7+ miles round trip and/or 2000+ feet vertical climb). This type of hike should only be undertaken if both dog and master are seasoned hikers and in excellent physical condition.

How the Trails Were Selected

What makes a dog-friendly hike? That depends on the dog. All of the trails in this book are dog-friendly, keeping in mind the trail rating. An old dog that enjoys a short "1 paw" (easy) route might find a 4-paw hike extremely unfriendly. But there are certain criteria that all hikes in this book meet.

First, it has to be a hike, not just a walk on a country road or in a town park. Hiking routes in New Hampshire and Vermont use woods roads, old carriage roads, historic bridle paths, former logging roads, and footpaths. Often they are a combination.

Second, while some of the trails in this book have short multi-use sections, they are primarily for foot traffic when snow is off the ground, and they are not open to motorized traffic, including ATVs and dirt bikes.

Third, dogs can negotiate the entire route, meaning no extensive boulder fields that require rock-hopping (with the exception of Mount Washington) and no long ladders or fixed ropes. The trails in northern New England are often rough, rocky, and eroded, but the ones in this book are all passable by a dog. The smallest breeds, such as Yorkies and pugs, might need a boost here and there, but otherwise there is no need to lift or lower a dog on any of these trails.

Fourth, with a few exceptions, the trails in this book were chosen because they are not crowded. And in the case of a popular mountain, the recommended route is usually the one less traveled.

Last but not least, the hike must have a human reward as well, usually a breathtaking view, because it must be a "best hike" for you as well as your dog.

As the title *Best Hikes with Dogs* suggests, most of the hikes in this book were chosen because they are simply awesome dog-hikes for all of the above reasons. However, in a few cases, mountains, ponds, or waterfalls are included because they are magnets for hikers. These destinations are considered among the best hikes in New Hampshire and Vermont, but not necessarily with dogs. Most people want to climb the well-known peaks like Mount Washington and Mount Chocorua in New Hampshire, and Camels

Opposite: White Ledge above the lily pads on Lake Solitude, Mount Sunapee

Hump and Mount Mansfield in Vermont, even if they are not particularly good choices with a dog. In those cases, this book gives a preferred route, even though the mountain would otherwise not qualify for the book.

Many people were consulted during the process of selecting the hikes in this book, including longtime local hikers, naturalists, rangers, trail workers, and representatives from the Appalachian Mountain Club and the Green Mountain Club—all who hike with dogs.

At the start of the project, the goal was a perfect 50–50 split between the two states and an equal number of hikes spread east to west and north to south. The reality is that some regions, such as the New Hampshire seacoast and extreme northwestern Vermont, do not have many hiking options, while others regions in the White Mountains and the Green Mountains are loaded with them. This book gives at least a couple of hikes in every part of both states. It also gives a range of hikes in terms of ability (distance and vertical gain) and destination (mountaintops, waterfalls, ponds). However, to get geographic distribution and a range of ability levels, a number of superb hikes have been omitted.

New Hampshire and Vermont are hiking-rich states. Upon completion of this book, I could have immediately written *Another 50 Incredible Hikes with Dogs: New Hampshire & Vermont*. However, none of the hikes on these pages will disappoint you. All are exceptional hikes for both you and your dog. Enjoy!

A Note About Safety

Safety is an important concern in all outdoor activities. No guidebook can alert you to every hazard or anticipate the limitations of every reader. Therefore, the descriptions of roads, trails, routes, and natural features in this book are not representations that a particular place or excursion will be safe for your party. When you follow any of the routes described in this book, you assume responsibility for your own safety. Under normal conditions, such excursions require the usual attention to traffic, road and trail conditions, weather, terrain, the capabilities of your party, and other factors. Keeping informed on current conditions and exercising common sense are the keys to a safe, enjoyable outing.

The Mountaineers Books

PART 2

New Hampshire

*From a dog's point of view, his master is an
elongated and abnormally cunning dog.*

*—Mabel Louise Robinson
Source: Dog Days, a Photographic Celebration
from the Hulton Getty Picture Collection
(Harper-Collins, 2000)*

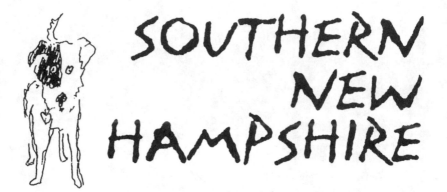

SOUTHERN NEW HAMPSHIRE

1. Lake Solitude—Mount Sunapee

Round trip: 4.8 miles

Hiking time: 3 hours

High point: 2700 feet

Elevation gain: 1507 feet

Difficulty: 2 paws (moderate)

Map: USGS Newport Quad

Location: Newbury, NH

Contact: Monadnock Sunapee Greenway Trail Club, *www.msgtc.org;*
New Hampshire Division of Parks and Recreation–Trails Bureau,
603-271-3254, *www.nhparks.state.nh.us*

Getting there: Take Route 103 south of Newbury. Turn onto Mountain
Road. The trailhead is about 1.2 miles up Mountain Road on the right,
just before a small bridge. The small sign is tucked into the trees, but
there is an obvious pullout for parking.

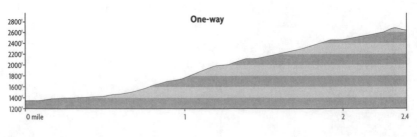

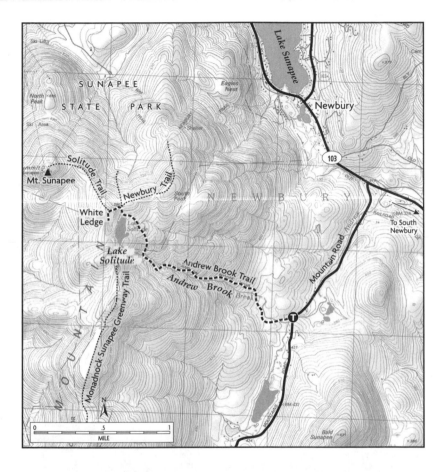

Located on a shoulder of Mount Sunapee, Lake Solitude and White Ledge above it are among the most peaceful hiking destinations in southern New Hampshire. White Ledge offers an arguably superior view compared to the top of the mountain, which is not above tree line, and it is definitely more of a wilderness experience. The summit is cluttered with two chairlift terminals, a sizable lodge, and several smaller buildings. During certain summer weekends, the Mount Sunapee ski resort offers chairlift rides, crowding the summit with people who have either ridden up or hiked up a ski trail. Unless you need to stand on top of the mountain, White Ledge is the preferable destination, particularly with a dog.

The Andrew Brook Trail follows an old, eroded woods road through a lush hardwood forest, crossing Andrew Brook several times. The first crossing is wide but shallow, easily fordable on stepping stones. The

Jason and Bravo enjoy the view of Lake Solitude from the top of White Ledge.

next crossing is via the only bridge. When the original bridge collapsed, the trail was rerouted around a small boulder and over a new narrower footbridge. It hooks back into the older, wider trail on the other side of the stream. The trail climbs gently, soon bending to the right (north) where a blue blaze (painted mark on a tree) and an arrow point the obvious way.

After a wider brook crossing, which can be challenging if the water is high, the trail continues to climb moderately at first, then steadily, next to the brook, passing a registration box. It levels off at about 1 mile, crossing the brook again, before ascending a short, steep pitch. Then it levels off again, passing a tributary brook on the right about a quarter-mile farther that has a chest-deep pool for retriever-size dogs. It is the best place for a dog to cool off between the trailhead and the lake, although your dog has many options. Water is plentiful along the entire route.

The next flat section is longer, traversing a muddy, wet area. Then the trail climbs moderately among more streamlets. The trail itself seems like a streambed, making it easy to confuse with the real streams, as the blazes are few. After about an hour of hiking, there is a noticeable change from hardwoods to softwoods. Old logs help you negotiate an extra-long muddy section if your balance is good.

The trail bends to the right around a small bog as it approaches Lake Solitude at 2 miles. Lake Solitude is technically a "tarn," a body of water found at higher altitudes. It is a scenic spot, with water lilies floating over much of the lake's surface, ducks diving for food, and a choir of frogs chirping loudly. Camping and campfires are not allowed at the lake.

White Ledge gleams 300 feet above the lake to the right. To reach it, walk along the shoreline to the intersection with the Monadnock–Sunapee Greenway (MSG, orange and white blazes). The MSG is approximately 50 miles long, from Grand Monadnock to Mount Sunapee. The original trail was laid out in 1921 by the Society for the Protection of New Hampshire Forests, the oldest and largest conservation group in the state. Turn right (north), heading upward onto drier ground. A little farther along, the MSG meets the Newbury Trail. Turn left (west), continuing on the MSG. Views of nearby hills appear through the trees to the left. After scrambling around a small boulder, the trail opens onto slab that is strikingly white. Bear left, walking across the top of the slab to White Ledge at 2.4 miles. The view is stunning, with the fire tower atop Mount Kearsarge visible to the east and a glorious expanse of hills and rural countryside extending south of Kearsarge as far as you can see.

Summit option: If you wish to climb to the ski area summit, bear right at the white slab, reentering the woods. The trail descends gently for about 0.7 mile until it reaches the "Upper Wing Ding" ski trail/work road. Turn left and follow the road to the summit. At the first ski-trail intersection, there is a nice view across Lake Sunapee. After a short, stiff climb up the work road, you will reach the summit at 3.4 miles. The best view is from the upper deck on the back side of the summit lodge. Lake Sunapee lies to the northeast. Mount Croydon with its white cliffs is straight ahead (north), and Mount Ascutney with its communication tower is to the west. It is a good idea to put your dog on a leash here as a courtesy to other people. Stay clear of the chairlifts, which can move at any time without warning. The total hike round trip is approximately four hours if you add the extra mileage from White Ledge to the summit.

2. North Pack Monadnock

Round trip: 4.6 miles

Hiking time: 3 hours

High points: 2290 feet (start of hike on the summit of South Pack Monadnock); 2278 feet (summit of North Pack Monadnock)

Elevation gain: 1570 feet

Difficulty: 2 paws (moderate)

Fees and permits: Day-use fee $3 per person

Pet policy: Leash pets within Miller State Park and on trail section owned by The Nature Conservancy

Maps: USGS Peterborough South Quad; USGS Peterborough North Quad; USGS Greenfield Quad

Location: Miller State Park; Peterborough, NH

Contact: New Hampshire Division of Parks and Recreation–Trails Bureau, (park) 603-924-3672, (South Region Office) 603-485-2034, *www.nhtrails.org;* The Nature Conservancy–New Hampshire Chapter, 603-224-5853, *www.nature.org*

Getting there: From Peterborough, take Route 101 east. Turn left into Miller State Park. From the tollbooth, drive up the auto road to the top of Pack Monadnock. The trailhead is on the northern end of the summit parking area.

"Pack" is a Native American word for "little." Compared to Grand Monadnock (elevation 3165 feet), its neighbor 12 miles to the west, Pack Monadnock is little, but it is still big for southern New Hampshire. Grand Monadnock may be a grand peak with an open, rocky top, but it is also closed to canines. Pack Monadnock is dog-friendly and still offers excellent views, as far as Manchester and Boston to the east, Mount Wachusett to the south, Mount Washington to the north, and Stratton Mountain to the west.

Pack Monadnock has three peaks, North, Middle, and South, all connected by the Wapack Trail. The south peak is in Miller State Park. The oldest state park in New Hampshire (established in 1891), it is named for General James Miller, a hero during the War of 1812 from nearby Temple, New Hampshire. The Wapack Trail, marked with yellow blazes, is a 21-mile footpath that starts at Mount Watatic in Massachusetts and ends at the trailhead on the northern side of North Pack Monadnock.

South Pack is accessible by a trail from the toll booth, but the more enjoyable hike with a dog begins at the summit and heads north. From the end of the parking circle, the Wapack Trail North descends gently over lengths of slab then enters a softwood forest. The trail bends right exiting the state park and immediately crosses a small streamlet as it continues its mellow descent. Your dog can now be leash-free, although you will want to keep the leash handy, as many people hike the trail with dogs.

At about 0.2 mile the trail passes a short spur to the right that leads to the "Joanne Bass Bross Memorial Scenic Outlook," named after a local conservationist. At the lookout, a rough rock bench is inscribed, "Joanne Bass Bross, 1915–2000. To walk these woods with you was to know no ordinary moment." The view east from the bench is not ordinary either. The panorama includes most of the southern New Hampshire plain.

From the lookout, the wide trail winds down the hillside. The footing is generally easy despite the numerous rocks, roots, and stretches of slab dotting the way, except for one slightly steeper eroded section.

At about 0.3 mile the trail flattens out across a mud hole, then arcs

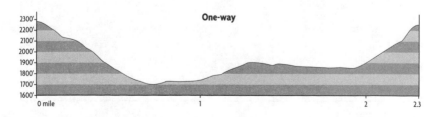

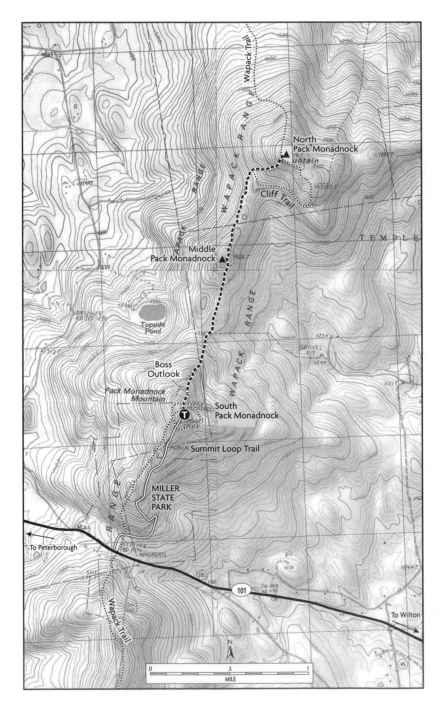

North Pack Monadnock

Cliff Trail

TEMPLE

WAPACK RANGE

Wapack Trail

PACK RANGE

Middle Pack Monadnock

Topside Pond

GRAVEL PIT

Boss Outlook

Pack Monadnock Mountain

South Pack Monadnock

T

Summit Loop Trail

MILLER STATE PARK

To Peterborough

Wapack Trail

101

To Wilton

N

0 .5 1
MILE

slightly left as it continues downhill. Soon it levels off again, now in a mixed forest with many birch and maple trees. It crosses an old stone wall into the Joanne Bass Bross Preserve, a 453-acre preserve owned and maintained by The Nature Conservancy. The trail traverses only about 100 yards of the preserve, mainly through a glade of tall spruce and fir trees. The rest of the route to North Pack Monadnock is in the Wapack National Wildlife Refuge, New Hampshire's first federal wildlife refuge. Established in 1972, it is a known hawk migration area. It also provides nesting habitat for numerous migratory songbirds such as the tree sparrow, Swainson's thrush, magnolia warbler, pine grosbeak, and white-throated sparrow. The refuge supports a wide variety of mammals as well, including deer, bear, coyote, fisher, fox, mink, and weasel, although the odds of an animal sighting are slim.

At about 0.8 mile the trail turns more noticeably upward over a short rise, then bends to the right. It crosses a large rock, then a wet area. Shortly afterward, it reaches a rock cairn in the middle of a slab clearing, which marks the top of Middle Pack Monadnock. Middle Pack is little more than a minor hump in the middle of the long saddle between South and North Pack. At 1.7 miles the trail comes to the junction with the Cliff Trail, which also goes to the summit of North Pack, but by a longer route. Bear left, staying on the Wapack Trail, which continues northeast traversing

Bravo checks out the large barrel-like cairn atop North Pack Monadnock.

the ridge. It crosses more slab as it passes through an airy spruce forest, then begins to climb gently.

Five minutes later the trail bends right, paralleling an old stone wall through a small swamp. The route is a little confusing in this section and not well marked. Bear left, mid-swamp, crossing the stone wall and climbing over more slab. The stone wall soon appears again on your right, to be crossed a second time. Then the trail and wall diverge. From here, the trail climbs again on a more sustained grade, though nothing extreme.

The trail angles up to the top, allowing a glimpse of South Pack through the treetops. It takes a sharp left, and you are there! The rocky top of North Pack is adorned with a large barrel-like cairn. Grand Monadnock is prominent to the west. There are also views of south-central New Hampshire, particularly of the Contoocook Valley, and of South Pack, with its fire and communications towers, 2.3 miles away.

3. Mount Kearsarge

Round trip: 2.9 miles
Hiking time: 3 hours
High point: 2937 feet
Elevation gain: 1117 feet
Difficulty: 2 paws (moderate)
Fees and permits: $3 per person (under 12 free), payable at entrance to Winslow State Park
Pet policy: Dogs are welcome but must be on leash in picnic area around trailhead
Map: USGS Andover Quad
Location: Winslow State Park; Wilmot, NH
Contact: New Hampshire Division of Parks and Recreation, 603-271-3556, *www.nhstateparks.org*

Getting there: From Interstate 89, take Exit 11 onto Route 11 east. Ignore the sign for Wadleigh State Park. Turn right at the sign for Winslow State Park on Kearsarge Valley Road. Turn right on Kearsarge Mountain Road, which winds upward to the toll gate.

There are actually two mountains called "Kearsarge" in New Hampshire, one in the town of Kearsarge near North Conway and the other in

Wilmot near New London. The former is officially referred to as "Mount Kearsarge North." This hike climbs the latter, known simply as "Mount Kearsarge."

The first Europeans to see Mount Kearsarge were likely members of an expedition led by Governor Endicott of the Massachusetts Bay Colony in 1652, who were looking for the source of the Merrimack River. Their map referred to the mountain as "Carasarga," or "notch-pointed mountain of pines" in the Native American language from which it was derived. The spelling "Kearsarge" first appeared in 1816 on a map of Merrimack County.

The summit of Mount Kearsarge is accessible from both Winslow State Park on its northwestern slope and Rollins State Park on its southeastern slope. While the Rollins side offers the quickest path to the top, a mere half mile from the parking lot, the Winslow side is worth the extra mileage. It is still a rather short hike and can be done as a loop, going up the Winslow Trail (1.1 miles to the summit) and down the longer Barlow Trail (1.8 miles to the parking lot). The parking lot offers a superb view, including Mount Sunapee (west), Ragged Mountain (north), and Pleasant Lake (northwest) with the ridge of the Green Mountains in the distance, but that is only a sneak preview of what awaits above.

Take the trail with the red blazes. As a result of its popularity, the Winslow Trail (also called the Wilmot Trail on one sign) is a wide thoroughfare, a classic New England mix of rocks and roots. Within the first ten minutes, the trail crosses a small stream. Water is plentiful for most of this hike during spring run-off or after periods of rain, but it is never reliable, so bring water for your pooch.

The trail climbs steadily southeast its entire way, with one steeper rockier section about halfway up. In this area, look for natural rock steps, which are easier on you and your dog. Allow your dog to zigzag up. Secure footing for boots and paws is never a question if you are observant. If the rock is wet and no one else is around, it is safer in this short section to allow your dog to find his own way up the rock, unattached to you.

About forty-five minutes into the hike, you will find a huge, sloping

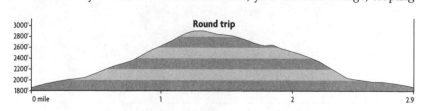

Round trip

boulder on your left. Deposited by the receding glacier of the last ice age, it is an excellent place to take a break and enjoy a view. Shortly afterward, you will glimpse the communication tower on the summit, then the fire tower beside it. It is a working fire tower with a ranger stationed inside. It is okay to climb the tower. Often the ranger will take a moment to say hello and allow you to look around from inside the lookout cabin, but if he is busy and the trap door is closed, remain below the door. Do not allow your dog to go up the fire tower!

The summit is bare as a result of a forest fire in 1796. It offers an

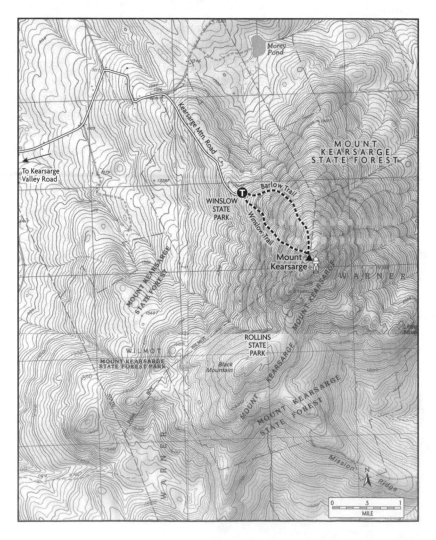

expansive 360-degree view. On most days, you can see the Green Mountains to the west and the White Mountains to the east. If it is very clear, you can see Boston and the Atlantic Ocean in the extreme distance to the south. There are also a couple of picnic tables in a sheltered notch in the rock just below the tower, the perfect lunch spot.

For the return trip, retrace your steps for 0.1 mile into the low, scrubby evergreens. At the sign, turn right onto the Barlow Trail (yellow blazes) and follow the rock cairns. Views to the north and west lie before you as the trail winds down off the summit. In mid-May there are hundreds of showy rhodora blooms along the sides of the trail. In early August it is worth pausing to pluck the tiny wild blueberries while you soak up more of the endless view.

Once in the trees, the Barlow Trail is very different from the Winslow Trail. It does not have as

Approaching the fire tower on Mount Kearsarge

much traffic, so it is less eroded, with more soil underfoot. With a gentler rate of descent and a softer landing with each step, the Barlow Trail is an easier way down on the knees.

LAKES REGION

4. Mount Major

Round trip: 3.4 miles
Hiking time: 3 hours
High point: 1784 feet
Elevation gain: 1180 feet
Difficulty: 2 paws (moderate)
Map: USGS West Alton Quad
Location: Alton Bay, NH
Contact: New Hampshire Division of Parks and Recreation,
603-271-3556, *www.nhtrails.org*

Getting there: The trailhead and parking are on Route 11, about 4 miles
north of Alton Bay, at the southern end of Lake Winnipesaukee.

The origin of the name Mount Major is a mystery. It does not refer to
the size of the mountain, but it might describe the view. The open bedrock summit perches over Lake Winnipesaukee, the largest lake in New
Hampshire. There are other hikes at the southern end of the lake, but
none with an expansive open top like Mount Major's.

Lake Winnipesaukee is home to a number of children's summer
camps, so there can be lots of people on the trails here, even midweek,

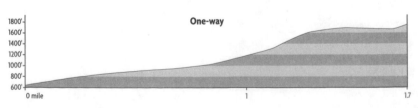

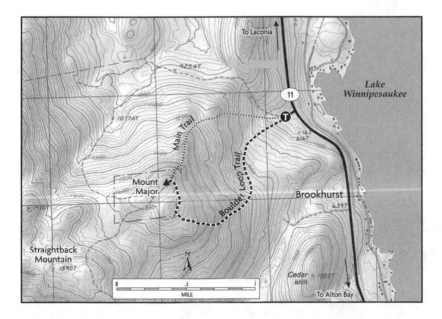

throughout the summer. And you are almost guaranteed to see other dogs. The best time to hike Mount Major is midweek after Labor Day, when school is back in session.

There are several trails up Mount Major. Most people take the Main Trail, but its upper section has lengthy stretches of steep rock, which can be slick when wet. With a dog, the Boulder Loop Trail (red blazes) is a better choice. It is generally less crowded and climbs on a dirt path most of the way. It does not hop from boulder to boulder, as the name implies, although some of the giant rocks add interest to the route.

The Boulder Loop Trail begins at the back left side of the parking lot. Turn 90 degrees upon entering the woods, then immediately bear right at the fork, heading uphill. The lower trail is wide like a woods road and well worn, through a hardwood forest.

The trail follows a streamlet, then crosses it just before a junction with the Beaver Pond Trail at about a quarter mile. Bear right, continuing uphill. After crossing a logging area, the trail bends left, then flattens on a long traverse before climbing gently again.

The route climbs over and around half-buried boulders, becoming somewhat rougher and more interesting. It becomes steeper as it winds up the hillside, passing over and beside more boulders. At one point, it actually crosses under a huge rock that is lodged next to a tree trunk.

A hug and a view of Lake Winnipesaukee from the rocky summit of Mount Major

Then, it scrambles up a short, ledgy area before bending right (north) at about 1.3 miles and leveling off on a height of land.

The trail crisscrosses some slab, then traverses on a smooth path through a pine glade. After the glade, it bends left over longer lengths of slab. The hill rolls away to the right as the trail arcs left past a narrow view of the lake. Soon there are constant views of the lake. The trail passes a small swamp on the left, then reaches the summit.

The remains of a stone hut mark the top, like a giant square cairn. The hut was built in 1925 by a former landowner, George Phippen, but the roof kept blowing off. Today, the stone walls still provide a haven from the wind.

5. Mount Percival–Mount Morgan Loop

Round trip: 5.5 miles
Hiking time: 4 hours
High point: 2238 feet (the Sawtooth, between Mounts Morgan and Percival)
Elevation gain: 1400 feet
Difficulty: 3 paws (ambitious)
Map: USGS Squam Mountains Quad
Location: Northern side of Squam Lake; northeast of Holderness, NH
Contact: Squam Lakes Association, 603-968-7336, *www.squamlakes.org*

Getting there: Take Route 113 north from Holderness. Park at the trailhead for Mount Morgan, the first and larger of the two trailheads, on the left, about 5.5 miles from Holderness.

Morgan and Percival are the mountain version of Siamese twins, connected at the shoulder. Both have open, rocky tops. Both can be hiked alone or together as a loop. If opting for the loop, the only argument for going up Percival and down Morgan is that the descent to your car is less steep, and shorter because the parking lot is at the base of Morgan.

From the parking lot, head up the Mount Morgan Trail (yellow blazes). At 0.1 mile turn right (northeast) on the Morgan–Percival Connector Trail. At 0.4 mile, turn left onto the Mount Percival Trail.

The Mount Percival Trail starts as a flat woods road. After passing through a small clearing filled with goldenrod and berries, it narrows to a footpath and starts to climb. After about twenty minutes, the trail bends right through a cut in a boulder, then heads east through a short sag before meandering back in a more northerly direction.

About a half hour into the hike, the trail crosses a stream with a small pool on the left. This is an excellent spot to let your dog cool off. It is

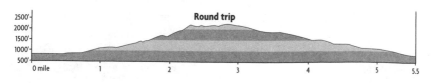

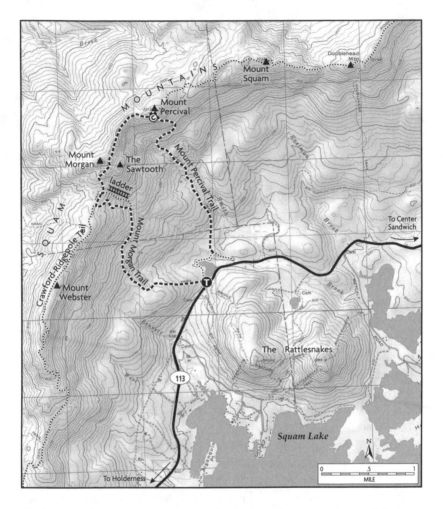

likely the only water on the trail if the weather has been dry, so definitely bring extra water for your dog on this hike.

The trail passes through a cut in an old stone wall before heading up more steeply. It bends left over a jumble of rocks, then crosses a swampy area on stepping stones. Stone steps aid the climb farther on, as you start to notice a gain in altitude.

Soon the trail becomes more eroded, resembling a dry streambed. But you are rewarded at 1.6 miles with your first open view. As you continue over a rocky outcropping, notice the shiny flecks of mica in the rock. After traversing through another rock jumble and going up a long series of stairs, the trail climbs more aggressively toward the top. It eventually reaches a section that is more of a scramble, but dogs seem to have little trouble here. Not so at the next intersection, if you take a wrong turn!

At 2.1 miles, at the base of a huge boulder, the trail comes to a fork. Take the right path to reach the summit over a series of rocky ledges. Avoid the left route, which sounds enticing—through a cave—but it is NOT dog-friendly, even for the most mountain-savvy dog. The cave is really a passage through a jumble of large rocks and boulders. Both routes end up at the summit at 2.2 miles, joining the Crawford-Ridgepole Trail.

The open, rocky summit of Mount Percival is a gem! Squam Lake is directly south, with larger Lake Winnipesaukee beyond, and crowned by Mount Major at the end of the lakes. To the right (west), you can see the ridge you are about to walk to Mount Morgan. Turn in the opposite direction to see a more mountainous view north of the Sandwich Range and Mount Chocorua in the distance.

From the summit of Mount Percival, bear left (west) onto the Crawford-Ridgepole Trail. The ridge trail is a lovely traverse through spruce trees and blueberry bushes. The footing varies between rock slab and soft soil. As you near the end of the ridge, the views come in rapid succession, first

Lucy finds a rock perch on Mount Percival.

to the right (north) of Mount Moosilauke then to the left (south) of the lakes, then ahead (due west) of the Tenney Ski Area.

At 2.9 miles the Crawford-Ridgepole Trail intersects with the Mount Morgan Trail. Turn right and continue a short 0.1 mile to the summit of Mount Morgan. The summit offers another outstanding view of Squam Lake and Lake Winnipesaukee. The big rocky peak to the southwest is Mount Cardigan. The fire tower visible on one of the closer mountains to the southeast is on Red Hill.

As with Mount Percival, there are options off the summit of Mount Morgan, one dog-friendly, the other not. This time, a lengthy ladder down a steep rock face on the Mount Morgan Trail is the problem. To avoid it, retrace a few steps back toward the ridge trail. Follow the ridge trail a little further, then take your next left.

As the Mount Morgan Trail nears its end, you will reach yet another intersection, this time with a logging road. Pay close attention to the yellow blazes in this area. Turn right on the road, then immediately left, back into the woods. After crossing another old rock wall, you will pass the intersection with the link to the Mount Percival Trail. From here, it is a short 0.1 mile to the car.

UPPER CONNECTICUT RIVER VALLEY

6. Black Mountain

Round trip: 4.5 miles
Hiking time: 3.5 hours
High point: 2836 feet
Elevation gain: 1800 feet
Difficulty: 2 paws (moderate)
Map: USGS East Haverhill Quad
Location: East Haverhill, NH
Contact: Black Mountain State Forest, 603-271-3456; *www.nhdfl.org*;
   White Mountain National Forest–Pemigewasset/Ammonoosuc
   District, 603-536-1315, *www.fs.fed.us/r9/white*

Getting there: From Route 25 in East Haverhill, turn north on Lime Kiln
Road. Go about 3 miles. Bear left at the fork. The trailhead is just after
the fork on your right.

Black Mountain is a rocky pyramid at the end of a long ridge called The
Hogsback. It is little known outside of the Upper Connecticut River Valley, perhaps because it is not a high peak, but it is a favorite among locals.

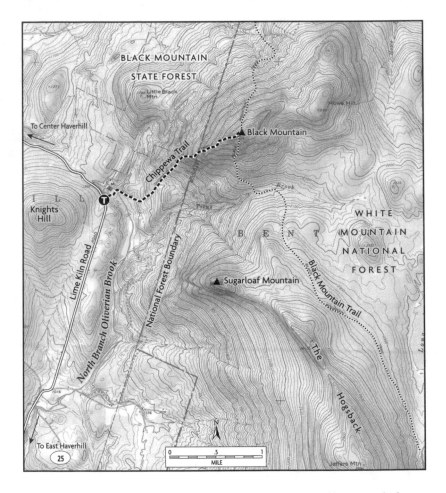

Expect to see a number of people with dogs on the trail, particularly on weekends.

The Chippewa Trail (sometimes called the Haverhill Heritage Trail; yellow blazes) dips down out of the parking lot, crossing a stream, then winds through the woods, quickly coming to a second stream, called North Branch Oliverian Brook. The path is wide and obvious, except at the brook. Cross the brook, keeping it on your left for a few steps, then leave it behind, as the trail heads up into the woods. A few minutes later, the trail meets a woods road. Turn right, following the road for about fifty paces, then turn left back onto the wide, smooth, road-like trail. It climbs gently, passing a hollow tree and begins paralleling a small stream on your right.

At about 1 mile, the undergrowth seems airier as the trail passes an overgrown rock foundation. Old stone walls zigzag through the woods. Tall pine and paper birch start to dominate as the trail begins a more serious ascent. As you climb, you can see ledgy Sugarloaf Mountain, farther south along The Hogsback. The trail heads northeast straight up the slope, interrupted only by periodic stone or wood steps and log water bars.

The footing gets rockier and the pines take over as the trail crosses onto state land. The path narrows and bends to the right, traversing a slope toward the south for a short way before reaching a switchback near a large boulder in the trees. From here, the ascent becomes steep again and rooted, as it climbs through a tall open grove of pine trees, more reminiscent of the Pacific Northwest than New England.

At about 1.6 miles the trail emerges on a large rocky outcropping, with a long view to the west into Vermont. It is a fun scramble up the rocks and slab above this lookout, as the trail weaves in and out of the trees. There are a number of viewpoints along the way, mainly into Vermont, but at the next rocky knoll Mount Moosilauke appears to the southeast, and Black's summit cone looms above.

At 1.9 miles the trail travels around the cone to an intersection with the Black Mountain Trail. It is a short scramble up the rocks onto the middle of the elongated summit ledge. Look left to Mount Lafayette and Franconia Ridge. The hulk of Mount Moosilauke lies straight ahead. The pyramid in the distance to the south is Mount Ascutney. Walk to the right through some low scrub to the end of the ledge for an expansive view to the east of Killington and the main ridge of the Green Mountains.

Black Mountain

7. Mount Cardigan

Round trip: 3 miles
Hiking time: 2 hours
High point: 3121 feet
Elevation gain: 1220 feet
Difficulty: 2 paws (moderate)
Pet policy: Need leash in picnic area by trailhead and around fire
    tower on summit
Map: USGS Mount Cardigan Quad
Location: Cardigan Mountain State Park; Orange, NH
Contact: New Hampshire Division of Parks and Recreation,
    603-271-3556, *www.nhstateparks.org*

Getting there: Take Route 4 to Canaan. Turn onto Route 118 north. Turn right onto Mountain Cardigan Road (also called Orange Road). Go past the Canaan Speedway, following the signs to Cardigan Mountain State Park & Forest. Park at the picnic area at the trailhead.

Mount Cardigan is one of the more popular hikes in this part of New Hampshire, so expect lots of kids, dogs, and other hikers on the trail. It is the perfect hike if you do not have a lot of time but want a big view, particularly if you and your dog are not frequent hikers. The view from the parking lot may tempt you to eat your picnic right there, but it is worth the walk up. With an expansive bald top, a fire tower, and a 360-degree view, it is hard to find a hike with a better reward for such a modest effort.

There are several ways to reach the summit, but the West Ridge Trail (orange blazes) is both dog-friendly and interesting. This well-maintained route begins with lots of stone-work and intermittent log and rock steps. The rocks are loaded with mica, which makes them sparkle in the sunlight.

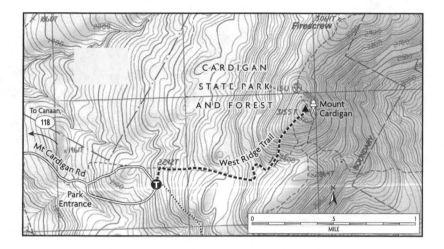

About 0.5 mile from the parking lot, the West Ridge Trail intersects with the South Ridge Trail. Turn left, staying on the West Ridge Trail. The trail climbs moderately, then flattens out, crossing two bridges over a large mud hole. It bends north (left), then heads up more steeply through a rocky area, past a small, picturesque waterfall on the left. Though the trail has more and more rock slab on it as you climb, the footing remains good.

At 1 mile the trail crosses a major footbridge over a stream. Shortly afterward, the trees begin to thin. The undergrowth turns to low blueberry bushes, then ends altogether as you break into the open.

Although technically not above tree line, the top of Mount Cardigan is a huge, bare dome thanks to a forest fire back in the 1800s. As you clear the trees, you feel like you are hiking to the sky. It takes about ten minutes to cross the rocky summit area to the fire tower on the top. The fire tower is usually closed, but you can climb the stairs. On a clear day, you can see Franconia Ridge to the east beyond Newfound Lake, with Mount Washington in the distance. Mount Sunapee (the ski area) and Mount Kearsarge (fire tower on top) lie to the south. Mount Ascutney dominates the western view.

Do not allow your dog to climb the fire tower! The steps are narrow, without risers, winding upward through scaffolding with little more than a thin metal handrail for protection. It is best to leave your dog on a leash with a friend below, or tied to the base of the tower, away from the stairs.

Descending from the summit of Mount Cardigan across the open bedrock

8. Mount Cube

Round trip: 6.6 miles
Hiking time: 4 hours
High point: 2909 feet
Elevation gain: 2200 feet
Difficulty: 3 paws (ambitious)
Map: USGS Piermont Quad
Location: Between Orfordville and Wentworth, NH
Contact: Dartmouth Outing Club (DOC), 603-646-2428,
   www.dartmouth.edu/~doc/

Getting there: From Route 10 in Orfordville, turn onto Route 25A. The trailhead is about 2 miles east of Mount Cube Farm, across the road from the Camp Moosilauke and Camp Merriweather soccer fields. Look for the brown and white Appalachian Trail sign on the right. Best parking is immediately after the trailhead in the wide turnout.

If you are looking for a little more mileage and vertical without overdoing it, Mount Cube is the perfect choice. With under 3000 feet of elevation,

Mount Cube may have less cachet than its larger neighbors, Smarts and Moosilauke, but it is still a terrific hike, especially with a dog. It offers solitude, abundant water (over a dozen stream crossings), and a great view from the top.

There is a chance you will see a bear on Mount Cube, because the mountain is within a designated rehabilitation area for orphaned cubs. Ben Kilham, a nationally renowned bear specialist, releases large cubs near Mount Cube to reintegrate them into the wild. If you see a bear with a collar or an ear tag, or if you think your dog might sense one, immediately put your dog on its leash, at heel, and keep walking. Make as much noise as possible by shouting and singing (see "Wildlife Encounters" in the introduction). Black bears are naturally timid and will likely depart for a quieter part of the forest. Some hikers have climbed Mount Cube annually for twenty-five years and have not seen a bear there, but it is worth noting the possibility, just in case.

The route described here follows the Appalachian Trail (white blazes), heading north to south. From the trailhead, it passes through a small swampy area, then crosses Brackett Brook, the first of numerous stream crossings. As with most of the streams on this hike, there is no bridge. Use some creative rock-hopping to get across.

Within minutes, the trail climbs gently to drier ground. The lower portion of the route is wide, with scattered rocks. It passes through a classic New England forest with mixed species of deciduous and coniferous trees and through several cuts in old rock walls. These rock walls, common throughout the lower woodlands in New Hampshire and Vermont, never had mortar. Dating back to the 1800s when large tracts of land were clear-cut for farming, the walls marked farm boundaries and confined livestock. Today, much of that land is now forest again. The trail passes the overgrown remnants of a stone foundation on the right, then crosses a gravel road at 0.5 mile, before becoming narrower and rooted.

About 1.5 miles into the hike, the trail takes a serious dip down and crosses Brackett Brook a second time. It is a substantial stream that turns

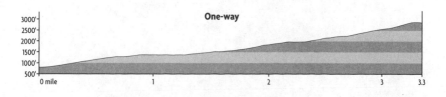

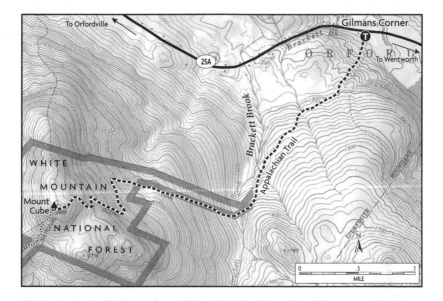

into a small river after a rainstorm. Normally, you can cross by hopping rocks that loosely connect one side of the brook to the other side, but if the water is high, look to the right (downstream) for a dry route by a birch tree perched in the middle of the water.

Ten minutes later the trail finally starts climbing in earnest, and it gets noticeably rockier. It can be slippery when wet, although the footing is greatly aided by many water bars and rock steps. It turns into a veritable stream after a heavy rain, so save this hike for a dry day unless you do not mind muddy paws in your car on the way home.

As the trail winds up the mountain, the trees become predominantly birch and spruce, which continue to shrink as you gain elevation. At about 3.1 miles, you will reach an intersection and sign pointing to the North Peak (right) or the South Peak (left). Go left (up). In less than five minutes, you will reach a short rock wall. Look left for the easiest route up the rock for both you and your dog. Beyond lies the summit with a superb view to the west of the Connecticut River Valley. Smarts Mountain is the dominant close peak on the left (southwest).

While this hike never really clears the tree line and while the summit is not completely bald, there is plenty of open rock. It is a great spot for a picnic, and for blueberry picking later in the summer.

Opposite: Lucy on the Appalachian Trail heading up Mount Cube

9. Moose Mountain

Total distance: 5.8 miles
Hiking time: 3 hours
High point: 2222 feet
Elevation gain: 1227 feet
Difficulty: 3 paws (ambitious)
Map: USGS Canaan Quad
Location: White Mountain National Forest; Hanover/Etna, NH
    (south trailhead) and Lyme (north trailhead), NH
Contact: Dartmouth Outing Club (DOC), 603-646-2428,
    www.dartmouth.edu/~doc/

Getting there, Goose Pond Road trailhead, Lyme (end of hike): Head north on Route 10 from Hanover toward Lyme. Turn right on Goose Pond Road. At the fork, bear left, continuing on Goose Pond Road. The trailhead is 3.5 miles on the right. Best parking is across the road from the trailhead. Leave one car here.

To Three Mile Road trailhead, Hanover/Etna (recommended start): In Etna, turn right on Rudsboro Road. Turn left on Three Mile Road. The trailhead is on the right. Best parking is across the road from the trailhead.

Moose Mountain is aptly named. The entire trail is prime moose habitat, with numerous swampy areas to the sides of the trail, although the trail itself is generally dry, soft dirt. Fresh moose tracks are virtually guaranteed, and moose sightings are common on the Moose Mountain Trail, part of the Appalachian Trail. The route is double-blazed, with both the standard white marking for the Appalachian Trail and orange blazes with a black stripe, the historical Dartmouth Outing Club (DOC) marking. Although

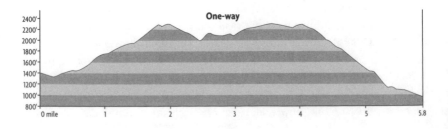

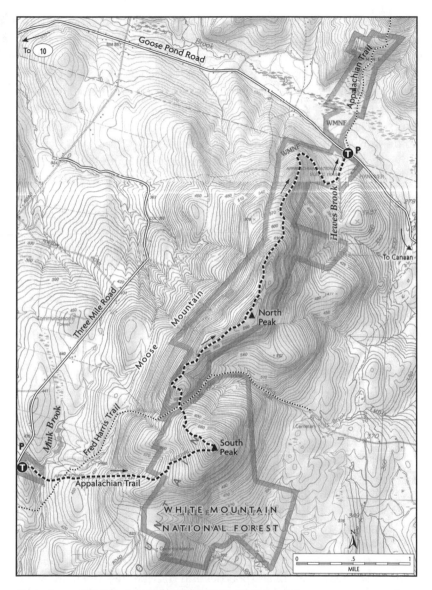

there is no leash law, your dog will definitely pick up a moose or deer scent at some point on this hike, so it is best to keep him on a leash if he has a propensity for tracking hoofed animals.

Moose Mountain is really a long ridge with two minor peaks. The taller South Peak is considered the main summit, but North Peak has the only view to the west. It is worth the trek over both peaks if you have two cars.

The route is described here from south to north, which is the more common direction, probably because thru-hikers on the AT go this way.

From the trailhead on Three Mile Road, the trail dips down over Mink Brook, where your dog will surely wade in, especially if your car ride was long. From the brook the trail ascends gently past an intersection with the Fred Harris Trail, named for the founder of the Dartmouth Outing Club. The foliage is lush, like a temperate jungle. In late May, trillium, columbine, and other wildflowers are abundant.

It takes about an hour of steady hiking to reach South Peak, 1.9 miles from the trailhead. The open, grassy top dates back to 1968, when it was cleared to allow a helicopter to evacuate victims of a plane crash. South Peak has a great view to the east across Goose Pond to Mount Cardigan. Have a picnic and turn around here if you want an easy, puppy-friendly outing.

Continuing onward from South Peak, the trail descends into a notch to a major intersection with the Wolfboro Road, an old unmaintained dirt road that looks more like a side trail. The old Moose Mountain Shelter used to be located to the right on Wolfboro Road, but it was demolished after the DOC constructed the new "Spruce Moose" Shelter in 2003, located 0.2 mile farther along the Appalachian Trail. This is also the second intersection with the Fred Harris Trail, which heads left. Go straight (north), following the sign in the direction of Holts Ledge and Trapper John Shelter to stay on the ridge heading toward North Peak.

From this intersection, the trail begins to climb moderately. It levels off under some low granite cliffs, then takes a couple of dips. It traverses a swampy area where stepping stones help keep feet dry. Let your dog lie down here to cool off; there is plenty of hike left for the mud to dry and fall off. The water source for the Spruce Moose Shelter is in this area, marked with blue blazes and a sign. Limit your dog to puddles that are not near the water source itself.

About forty minutes after leaving the South Peak, the trail heads up for the last time. As it flattens there are glimpses of the next mountain ridge to the east through the leaves. This stretch of trail is berry-heaven, with an abundance of wild raspberries and strawberries. The trees, while still overhead, become noticeably shorter and more sporadic.

At about 3.4 miles, the trees suddenly become predominantly pine. You will come upon a rocky outcropping on the left, surrounded by a sea of blueberry bushes. This is North Peak. It is unmarked but obvious a few steps later, as the trail begins to descend steadily and the flora reverts to ferns and hardwoods again.

The final lookout, and the nicest view of the hike, is another 0.2 mile farther. The fire tower on top of Smarts Mountain dominates the northeastern landscape, with Mount Cube to the left along the same ridge.

The trail continues downhill through another grove of pines, then angles to the right. It crosses Hewes Brook, a reliable water source and a welcome spot for your dog to take another dip (and for you to wash off the mud, if there is any left). The trail follows the brook, leveling off about a half mile from the end of the hike at Goose Pond Road.

Bridge over Mink Brook on Moose Mountain

10. Mount Moosilauke

Round trip: 7.2 miles
Hiking time: 4.5 hours
High point: 4802 feet
Elevation gain: 3110 feet
Difficulty: 4 paws (strenuous)
Map: USGS Mount Moosilauke Quad
Location: White Mountain National Forest; Benton, NH
Contact: Dartmouth Outing Club (DOC), 603-646-2834,
    www.dartmouth.edu/~doc/; Appalachian Mountain Club (AMC),
    603-466-2721, *www.outdoors.org*; White Mountain National Forest–
    Pemigewasset/Ammonoosuc District, 603-536-1315,
    www.fs.fed.us/r9/white

Getting there: From Route 112, just east of the intersection with Route 116, turn onto Tunnel Brook Road. Bear left at the fork and continue another 1.5 miles to the trailhead on the left.

Mount Moosilauke is the dominant mountain in this part of New Hampshire and the spiritual center of the Dartmouth Outing Club (DOC), which maintains its trail network as well as the 50-mile stretch of Appalachian Trail from Hanover to Moosilauke. It is a hulk of a peak with a sprawling, open summit. At 4802 feet, it is ranked tenth among the forty-eight peaks in New Hampshire over 4000 feet.

The first official ascent of Mount Moosilauke was by the moose hunter, Chase Whitcher, in 1773. However, the name "Moosilauke" has nothing to do with the large, hoofed beast common to its slopes. It is derived from the Abenaki Indian words "moosi" and "auke," which mean "bald place." About 100 acres of the mountain are above tree line, leaving hikers exposed in bad weather. Always bring warm clothes on

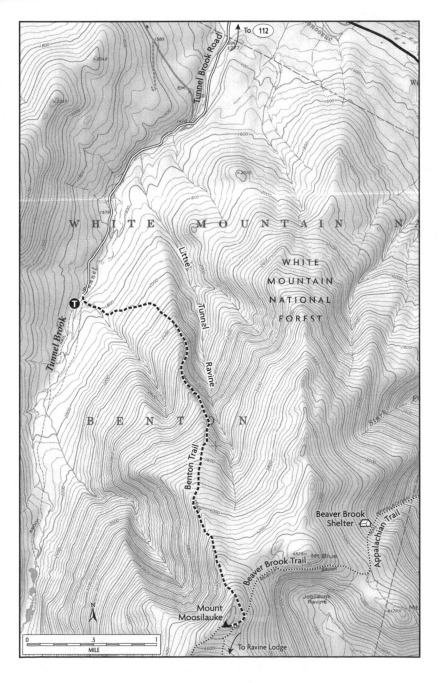

Above tree line on Mount Moosilauke

this hike, even if it is 85 degrees and sunny at the trailhead.

There are a half dozen ways to hike Moosilauke, all of them interesting, but the Benton Trail (blue blazes) is the best with a dog, particularly if your dog is not the valedictorian of obedience school. It is one of the least used routes due to its location on the opposite side of the mountain from the Moosilauke Ravine Lodge, a sizable, dog-friendly log building with several nearby bunkhouses, owned by Dartmouth College, and the starting point for over half of the other routes up the mountain. In addition, the Benton Trail is relatively easy and more scenic than the routes from the Ravine Lodge.

From the trailhead, turn right as you enter the woods on an old logging road. Tunnel Brook, which is closer to a small river than a brook, will be on your left. Shortly after entering the woods, the trail crosses the brook via large rocks and stepping stones, which can be under a torrent during spring run-off or other high-water times. Once over the brook, the trail climbs steadily, crossing an old logging road as you ascend through an open hardwood forest. Be sure to carry water for your dog. After crossing Tunnel Brook, the Benton Trail is dry except for the occasional lucky puddle and one spring quite high on the mountain.

About 1 mile up, the trees become predominantly spruce and hemlock and the footing changes from scattered rocks to soft soil and roots. There is a break in the trees on the right at 1.3 miles, with a view into Little Tunnel Ravine (below) and of the Kinsman Range to the left (north). Once on the ridge, the trail climbs in waves. As the trees thin out, a lawn of wood sorrel and moss stretches out from the trail on either side.

At 3.2 miles the Beaver Brook Trail (Appalachian Trail) merges with the Benton Trail. If you are backpacking, the Beaver Brook Shelter is 1.9 miles to the left. To reach the summit, go straight, following the white blazes and rock cairns another 0.4 mile. From this point on, you are in a fragile alpine zone. Camping is not allowed. You and your dog must stay on the trail, so a leash is highly recommended.

Once above the trees, you feel like you have been transported to a distant alpine land. The trail crosses the expansive summit plateau, affording some of the most magnificent views in New Hampshire and Vermont. To the northeast, the layers of tall ridges culminate at Mount Washington and the Presidential Range. The bare peaks and steep slides of Franconia Ridge are behind you on the way up and in your face on the way down. The high peaks of the Adirondacks lie to the west across the Connecticut River Valley.

11. Smarts Mountain

Round trip: 7.1 miles
Hiking time: 5.5 hours
High point: 3238 feet
Elevation gain: 2400 feet
Difficulty: 4 paws (strenuous)
Map: USGS Smarts Mountain Quad
Location: Lyme Center, NH
Contact: Dartmouth Outing Club (DOC), 603-646-2428,
   www.dartmouth.edu/~doc/; White Mountain National Forest–
   Pemigewasset/Ammonoosuc District, 603-536-1315,
   www.fs.fed.us/r9/white

Getting there: From Route 10 in Lyme, follow Dorchester Road through Lyme Center toward the Dartmouth Skiway. Just before the Skiway, bear

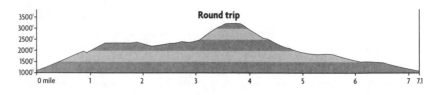

left at the fork, continuing on Dorchester Road, which turns to dirt. From the fork, the trailhead is 1.7 miles on the left.

Smarts Mountain is not a 4000-footer, but it feels like it when you climb it. The mountain is a large, flat-topped dome when viewed from the Hanover area. Although the summit is covered with trees, it has a tall fire tower, and the approach via the Lambert Ridge Trail (Appalachian Trail, white blazes) gets you up high quickly with numerous ledgy vistas en route to the top. Bring extra water for your dog, because there are no reliable streams on the way up the Lambert Ridge Trail.

Many people like to hike both ways on the Lambert Ridge Trail, because it is on a ridge, with wonderful views. There are three reasons for descending via the Ranger Trail. First, to make a loop. Second, because the bottom third of the trail is smooth and flat, so it is easier on the joints—both yours and your dog's. And third, for the water. The Ranger Trail crosses a large brook about halfway down, then follows it much of the way to the trailhead. Your dog will welcome the chance to get refreshed. And if mileage matters, the Ranger Trail is 0.3 mile shorter than the ridge route.

Smarts Mountain is in the heart of a bear rehab zone. Although rare, radio-collared bears are sometimes seen from the trail. If you see a bear, do not run. Put your dog on a leash, make a lot of noise, and wave your arms, without looking directly at the bear. The bear will likely run away. (For more on how to handle bear encounters, see "Wildlife Encounters" in the introduction.)

Begin at the trailhead near the entrance to the small parking lot. (You will exit via the trailhead at the back of the parking lot.) The Lambert Ridge Trail winds up the hillside through a mixed hardwood forest, soon passing between two boulders and crossing an old stone wall. After a series of stone steps, there is a narrow view of the neighboring hillside to the right, but five minutes later, at 0.8 mile, the trail reaches a length of open ledge and the first real view. You have gained the first "step" of the ridge. Look back over your shoulder to see Holts Ledge and the Dartmouth Skiway.

The trail continues to climb, more gently now, traversing two more open ledges. Both allow views to the south across Reservoir Pond to Mount Cardigan in the distance. After the third lookout, the trail bends left back into the woods. Although viewless, it is a lovely walk, much of it across open slab, with a vivid patchwork of moss and lichen to the sides of the path.

At about 1 mile the trail ascends rather steeply again to another long stretch of slab. Then it eases and bends left, following several small cairns as it traverses the main ridge. At about 1.4 miles, there is a narrow view through the trees to the north. The altitude is noticeably higher as spruce and hemlock now line the trail.

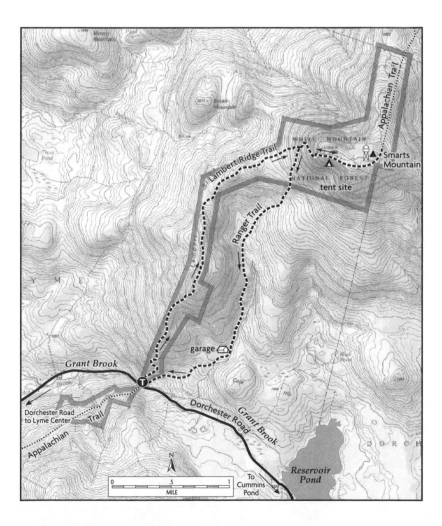

At 1.8 miles the trail crosses another ledgy lookout, with a view of the summit almost 2 miles away, as well as the hills to the southeast. From here, the trail crosses more slab and ledge, then descends into a shallow col between the ridge and the summit cone. The long traverse continues, but now through a low-lying, muddy area, often dotted with moose tracks. In this area, at the first sign that your dog has a nose-full of animal scent, you should put her on a leash.

After crossing a series of split-log footbridges through a particularly muddy area, the trail begins to climb again, moderately at first. After several stone steps, the climb becomes persistent, helped by more stone steps but hindered by stretches of wet bedrock where the thin soil has worn away.

At 3.3 miles the Lambert Ridge Trail meets the Ranger Trail. Turn left, continuing steadily upward across more wet rock. The trail from here to the top is old and well used. There are several tricky sections where the trail has eroded down to granite slab, but agile dogs, with their lower centers of gravity, will have no problem. It is undeniably a steep slog to the summit from the junction with the Ranger Trail, broken only by a periodic bend in the path or a few stone steps, but at about 3.5 miles the grade eases across a stretch of slab. The trees get shorter, and the canopy breaks.

At 3.7 miles the trail reaches the summit plateau. A short spur to the right goes to a tent site, a small grassy clearing with a fire ring and a superb view of Mount Cardigan to the south. Many people like to climb Smarts just to camp at this perch. There is no water at the tent site, but a spring, located about 0.2 mile north of the summit on a blue-blazed spur, is usually reliable. If you decide to camp here, it is advisable to carry enough water for you and your dog for the duration of your stay.

The spur makes a loop back to the main trail. Once there, turn right, continuing toward the northeast. The trail dips slightly as it winds around the base of the fire tower. The best access to the tower is around the bend to the left.

The base of the fire tower takes up most of the clearing where it stands. There is no view from the bottom, but from the top it is among the best in the state south of Mount Moosilauke. On a clear day, you can see Mount Ascutney to the south, the main ridge of the Green Mountains to the west, and Franconia Ridge and the Presidential Range to the east and north.

As with many old fire towers in New Hampshire and Vermont, bits of glass may be scattered around the base of the tower, due to broken windows. Watch where your dog steps. And never take your dog up the fire tower! To complete the loop, retrace your steps back to the junction with the Lambert Ridge Trail at 4.1 miles, but continue straight ahead on the Ranger Trail. After an initial drop from the junction, the pitch moderates. The path is worn down to slab for much of the descent, so it is smooth going, but it can be very slippery when wet.

As the grade eases, the trail becomes more rock-strewn, like a dry streambed, which in fact it is, just before crossing a real stream at about 5 miles. Your dog will appreciate the water, the first of any note since leaving the car.

From the stream, the trail smooths out, descending effortlessly to a larger stream, a tributary to Grant Brook, at 5.2 miles. An odd one-stall garage stands in the forest across the larger stream at the end of an old woods road. Cross the stream and turn left by the garage. From there, it is a gradual 1.9-mile descent to the parking lot, paralleling the stream the entire way.

Bravo pauses on a ledgy lookout on the Lambert Ridge Trail; a view of the summit of Smarts Mountain lies behind him, capped by a cloud.

THE WHITES

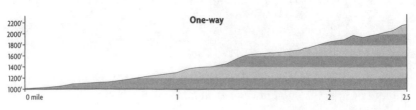

12. Bridal Veil Falls

Round trip: 5 miles
Hiking time: 3 hours
High point: 2200 feet
Elevation gain: 1200 feet
Difficulty: 2 paws (moderate)
Maps: USGS Sugar Hill Quad; USGS Franconia Quad
Location: Franconia, NH
Contact: White Mountain National Forest–Pemigewasset/
Ammonoosuc District, 603-869-2626, *www.fs.fed.us/r9/white*

Getting there: From Franconia, take Route 116 south. Turn left on Coppermine Road, 1 mile past the Franconia Inn. Park immediately on the left in a pullout before the "Private Road" sign. There is no sign for the trailhead, only the pullout.

Bridal Veil Falls is a scenic cascade on the northwestern side of a ridge between Cannon Mountain and The Cannon Balls. It is one of the most beautiful waterfalls in New Hampshire. Coppermine Brook pours through a narrow spot in a high ledge, then widens as it plummets, resembling the shape and color of a bride's long, lacy veil. The approach to the falls is a pretty hike. It follows Coppermine Brook most of the way, which has numerous pools that will delight your dog.

From the parking area, walk up the dirt road a short way to a fork.

One-way

2200'			
2000'			
1800'			
1600'			
1400'			
1200'			
1000'			
0 mile	1	2	2.5

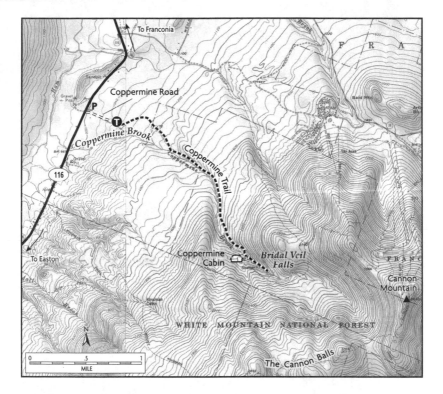

Bear right at the fork, following a sign that says "foot travel only." At about 0.4 mile, a brown sign with a hiker symbol marks the start of the Coppermine Trail (yellow blazes). Turn left into the woods.

At about 0.6 mile at an intersection, a blue sign points straight ahead for the "Coppermine Trail to Bridal Veil Falls." Follow the sign, ignoring the other trail, which departs to the right to a dead end.

At about 0.8 mile, the trail rises steadily into a stand of evergreens. Coppermine Brook is now an audible rush below. The path is broad and soft, covered with pine needles. It passes a primitive campsite on the right, then comes to a fork with one of the Franconia Inn's cross-country ski trails. Bear right.

The trail becomes rockier and soon crosses a streamlet, where your dog will likely want to pause. But a better spot is just a little farther down the trail. By 1 mile, the trail meets Coppermine Brook again. If the water is low, there is a pool here, where your dog can take a dip.

The trail veers away from the stream now and again, climbing at a moderate rate. At about 1.6 miles, the trail arcs left, leaving the brook

Bridal Veil Falls

for a longer time. It climbs up a steep slope, then eases, passing through a lovely area where the leaves hang like lace over the trail.

The brook appears again on the right, just as the trail goes up another brief steep section. A few moments later, at 2.3 miles, the trail crosses the brook on a constructed bridge. It climbs gently up the opposite side of the brook. The surrounding woods are littered with boulders capped with large trees that grow off them at odd angles, their roots snaking down to the thin soil below.

At 2.4 miles the trail comes to the Coppermine Cabin, a lean-to perched on the side of the brook. The shelter is maintained by the Forest Service and is available on a first-come, first-served basis. Cross behind the shelter, and you are basically there. If you continue to step rock-to-rock (dogs will wade and love it), you can work your way to a spit of land that splits the brook. There is another primitive campsite on the left. The trail ends at a large pool, but you can get closer to the waterfall by crossing the right branch of the brook and carefully making your way up the slippery rock to the last pool at the base of the cascade.

13. Carter Dome–Mount Hight Loop

Round trip: 10.2 miles
Hiking time: 7 hours
High point: 4832 feet
Elevation gain: 3600 feet
Difficulty: 4 paws (strenuous)
Map: USGS Carter Dome
Location: Between Gorham, NH and Pinkham Notch
Contact: Appalachian Mountain Club (AMC), 603-466-2721, *www.outdoors.org;* White Mountain National Forest–Androscoggin Ranger District, 603-466-2713, *www.fs.fed.us/r9/white*

Getting there: From Gorham, head south on Route 16 toward Pinkham Notch. Park at the trailhead for 19-Mile Brook Trail on the east (left) side of the road, just north of the Mount Washington Auto Road.

The Carter Dome–Mount Hight Loop is less crowded and less of a boulder pile than its Presidential neighbors across Route 16, which makes it appealing for dog owners. It is a long hike, but with several rewards, including exceptional mountaintop views and a lovely mountain lake.

Carter Dome is presumably named for Dr. Ezra Carter, who explored

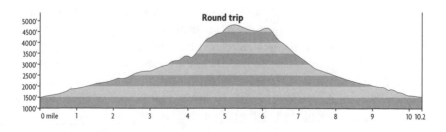

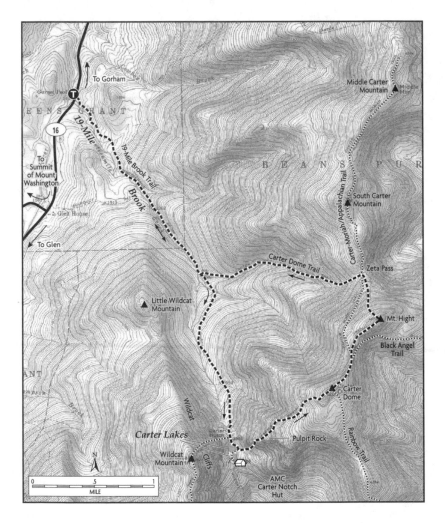

the White Mountains in the 1800s looking for medicinal herbs. It is ranked ninth among the 4000-footers of the White Mountains. Mount Hight is named for Dr. Carter's hiking companion from nearby Jefferson, New Hampshire. Although well above 4000 feet, Mount Hight (elevation 4675 feet) is considered a sub-peak of Carter Dome, rather than a 4000-footer in its own right, yet it seems a distinct peak when hiking the ridge between the two. Ironically, the taller Carter Dome has a broad, flat summit area with limited views through the scrub trees, whereas the shorter Mount Hight is capped by an open, rocky pinnacle and thus offers the better unobstructed panoramas.

A number of guidebooks lead hikers up Mount Hight first, but with a dog it is best to go in the opposite direction. There is a long, steep pitch from Carter Notch to the summit of Carter Dome that is more dog- and people-friendly to ascend, rather than descend, especially if pooch or person has any joint issues.

From the trailhead, enter the woods on the 19-Mile Brook Trail. As you would expect, the wide trail follows 19-Mile Brook, which seems like a small river. Although the path starts out on the rocky side, it immediately smooths out and begins a gentle ascent. There are several shallow pools along the way to Carter Notch where your dog can take a dip (although you might want to wait until the way out). There is a lot of water and several bridge crossings on the lower portion of this hike, as a number of mountain streams merge with 19-Mile Brook.

At 1.8 miles, the trail comes to a fork. The Carter Dome Trail exits to the left (east), which will be your return route. Bear right (southeast), continuing on 19-Mile Brook Trail, up a few stone steps and across a log bridge. The path becomes steeper but still nothing serious, and soon follows, then crosses another brook.

About five minutes later, the trail levels off again, crossing some slab and a few streamlets that are much less substantial than the brook and its tributaries below. In another five minutes the trail crosses yet another bridge and climbs a dozen stone steps. Then it gets steeper again and resembles a streambed itself. Spruce trees take over.

At 3.3 miles the trail comes to a T. The impressive 1000-foot Wildcat Cliffs tower above you and the Wildcat Ridge Trail exits to the right, heading west. Turn left (south), remaining on the 19-Mile Brook Trail, which is now also the Appalachian Trail (white blazes), and head down to the larger of the two Carter Lakes.

Plan a break by the lake. It is truly a dramatic setting, with the cliffs above and a plethora of wildlife below. Trout rise among the lily pads. Great blue herons wade along the banks. Ducks dive for their dinner. And although the hike to this point has been relatively easy, you have completed a third of the trip, so Rover will likely want to go for a swim.

The trail becomes the Carter–Moriah Trail at the lake. It goes around the left side of the lake, turning uphill just before reaching the AMC Hut at Carter Notch, which is actually several small buildings, including the main hut and two bunkhouses. As dogs are not allowed in the hut, and as it can be a busy place, it is best to skip taking the short spur there. If you choose to check it out, put your dog on a leash.

At 3.5 miles, the trail leaves the lake behind and the real climb begins. From the lake, it is a heart-pounding ascent, over 1400 feet in only 1.2 miles, on an eroded trail that seems particularly arduous after the long, flat approach to the lake. However, there are several places along the climb to catch your breath, if only to lose it again when you take in the view. When the canopy breaks, look back at Mount Washington, with its auto road lying like a silvery ribbon along its side. The green roof of Carter Notch Hut peek out from the narrow ravine below you.

At 3.8 miles, a short spur to the right leads to Pulpit Rock, a small perch over a precipitous drop. The view across the Wildcat River Valley is magnificent and worth the look, but only if your dog is tightly controlled on a leash. Better yet, leave your dog with a fellow hiker on the main trail.

Hikers pause with their dog at the larger Carter Lake below the Wildcat Cliffs.

After the next knoll, the path climbs at a more reasonable rate and the footing gets better, as it heads in a northeasterly direction. At this point, there are continuous views of Mount Washington and the northern Presidentials on your left through the low spruce trees.

At a substantial cairn, shaped like a cone, the trail bends to the right, then opens onto the summit of Carter Dome at 5.2 miles. The footings of an old fire tower that was removed in 1947 dot the elongated clearing, which offers limited views, mainly of Gorham to the north at the far end of the summit area.

From Carter Dome the trail descends into a saddle, reaching a double intersection at 5.6 miles. The Black Angel Trail departs to the right, then a few paces later the trail forks. If the weather is bad, take the left fork, bypassing the summit of Mount Hight. Otherwise bear right, staying on the Carter–Moriah/Appalachian Trail.

The trail heads north, dipping down, then flattening again. It passes through a mud hole, then climbs gradually to the top of Mount Hight where there is a 360-degree view. The Baldfaces are immediately to the east beyond the Wild River Valley. The ever-present Presidential Range dominates to the west. The rest of Carter Ridge trails off to the north, and Conway Lake shines to the south.

At the summit of Mount Hight, the trail takes a sharp left toward Mount Washington. It is a short scramble over a few boulders, then a more normal, though steep descent to a junction where the Carter–Moriah Trail and the Carter Dome Trail merge together.

The trail eases into a less joint-jarring descent, reaching Zeta Pass at 6.4 miles. Zeta Pass is marked by a log bench and another fork, where the Carter–Moriah Trail and Carter Dome Trail split again. Bear left on the Carter Dome Trail.

The trail winds down to a cascading brook, the first water since the two summits and a good place for a doggie break. Cross the brook on stepping stones and continue to descend, passing through a confluence of streams. The deeper second pool is particularly dog-appealing. The path follows this brook back to the 19-Mile Brook Trail, closing the loop.

14. Mount Chocorua

Round trip: 7.6 miles
Hiking time: 6 hours
High point: 3475 feet
Elevation gain: 2250 feet
Difficulty: 4 paws (strenuous)
Fees and permits: $3 parking fee at the trailhead drop box (bring exact change)
Map: USGS Mount Chocorua Quad
Location: Between Passaconaway and Conway, NH
Contact: White Mountain National Forest–Saco Ranger District, 603-447-5448, *www.fs.fed.us/r9/white*

Getting there: Take Route 112 (the Kancamagus Highway) 20 miles east of Lincoln or 11.5 miles west of Conway. The trailhead and parking lot are on the south side of the road.

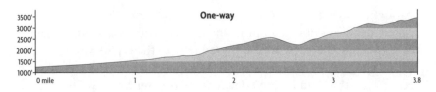

Although it is not a 4000-footer, Mount Chocorua is one of the most popular "big mountain" hikes in the White Mountains due to its vicinity to North Conway and the fact that its summit is a spectacular pinnacle of open granite. Expect to meet lots of other hikers and dogs, particularly on the Champney Falls Trail, described here, which is the most dog-friendly way to reach the peak. Be forewarned, the granite on the upper mountain has a reputation for tearing paw pads, so avoid this climb completely until your dog's pads are conditioned to strenuous hiking. Even if your dog is a seasoned mountain climber, it is a good idea to carry a doggie first-aid kit and a set of dog booties on this outing.

The Champney Falls Trail and the falls themselves are named for Benjamin Champney, a noted nineteenth-century artist in the White Mountains. From the trailhead, the trail crosses Twin Brook, then immediately comes to an intersection with the Bolles Trail. Go straight, heading south. After about fifteen minutes of easy walking, the trail meets Champney Brook, but does not cross it. Rather, it heads up gently, paralleling the brook, and soon rises well above it. The trail is open here, under tall hemlocks, with a mosaic of exposed roots to either side.

At 1.4 miles, the spur to Champney Falls leaves to the left. Champney Falls could be a destination in its own right, if you are not feeling up to a major climb. If the summit is your goal and if you are pressed for time, go straight, avoiding the falls. Otherwise, follow this scenic detour, which loops back into the main trail 0.3 mile farther up the mountain.

Champney Falls is a 70-foot series of cascades, which can be a magnificent rush or a minute trickle, depending on the season and the weather. If the cascades are calm, the small pool at the bottom is an excellent spot for your dog to cool off. The loop trail climbs up the right side of the falls before rejoining the main trail.

Back on the main trail, as you gain altitude, you begin to get glimpses to the left (east) of Middle Sister, the round, rocky peak that is on a shoulder of Chocorua. At 2.4 miles, just after the first real scenic vista, the trail bends to the right, heading up through a series of long switchbacks that lead to an upper ridge of the mountain. This part of the trail

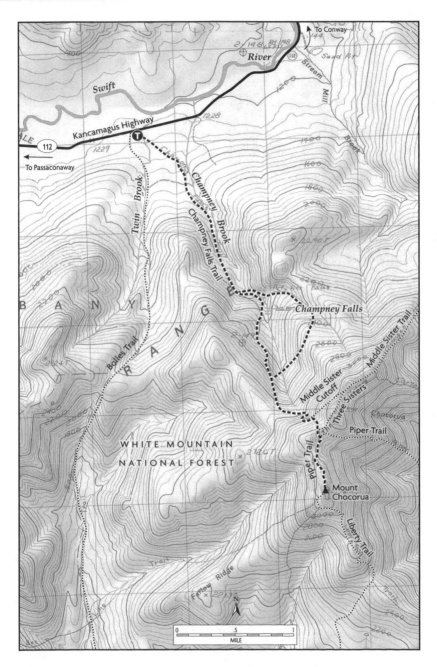

Taking a break on the Champney Falls Trail on Mount Chocorua

has a lot of side-hill slab and can be slippery when wet, but there are usually flat spots to step on if you pay attention. This is a good place to take your dog off his leash so that you both can independently pick your footing without an un-expected tug.

At 3 miles the trail meets the Champney Falls Cutoff to Middle Sister, the first of several intersections between here and the summit. Turn right toward Mount Chocorua. At 3.2 miles bear right again at the intersection with the Middle Sister Trail, continuing south on level ground and crossing more slab. As you round the bend, the summit cone of Chocorua looms ahead above the trees.

The next intersection marks the end of the Champney Falls Trail at the Piper Trail (yellow blazes). Bear right again. At 3.4 miles the West Side Trail enters from the left, but stay right on the Piper Trail. The trail remains flat through a spruce corridor, then leaves the trees.

From here to the summit, it is a fun scramble over expanses of rock. With each knoll, the mountain offers another tremendous view, but pay attention to the route, which is easy to lose on the open rock. When you do pause, the Cranmore Mountain Resort is visible to the northeast. Over the next rise, Franconia Ridge appears to the northwest. Then the trail bends up over another rocky outcropping, revealing the entire Lakes Region. Any point above tree line is a fine place to stop. In fact, unless you and your dog are comfortable climbing on steep rock, call this your destination. And if the top is crowded, this area is a better spot for a picnic.

For seasoned peak-baggers, the final knob of rock looks sheer, but it is accessible if you follow the trail to the right, where it meets the Liberty

Trail. Turn left at this narrow intersection, climbing up the rocks. All of the routes up Mount Chocorua funnel into this point, so it can be a bottleneck, yet it is difficult to keep your dog on a leash here because you both need to climb agilely. This section of the climb is only appropriate for dogs that are not only expert climbers, but also well socialized among both people and other dogs. Again, check your dog's pads frequently for cuts. The texture of the rock is like prickly sandpaper.

15. Kilburn Crag

Round trip: 1.4 miles
Hiking time: 1 hour
High point: 1300 feet
Elevation gain: 210 feet
Difficulty: 1 paw (easy)
Pet policy: Dogs must be leashed at all times. Owners must clean up after their dogs.
Map: USGS Littleton Quad
Location: Littleton, NH
Contact: Littleton Area Chamber of Commerce, 603-444-6561, *www.littletonareachamber.com/info/outdooractivities.cfm*

Getting there: From Interstate 93, take Exit 43 "Littleton, Dalton." Turn right off the ramp onto Route 135 south. Take your first right onto St. Johnsbury Road (Route 135 and Route 18). The trailhead is on the left, 0.4 mile from the turn. Park at the trailhead.

Kilburn Crag is a rocky outcropping on the northeastern shoulder of modest Walker Mountain. It is known mainly to Littleton locals. With easy footing and low mileage, it is a perfect hike for puppies or senior

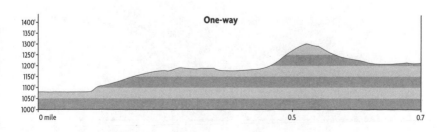

dogs and a good choice if you are just getting your hiking legs, short on time but in need of a decent view, or if you simply want some quality time in the woods with your pooch without committing to an epic outing.

From the trailhead, the smooth, wide trail—a "woods road" if it were in the woods—crosses a field, then enters the forest, on a steady incline. At about 0.3 mile it passes a bench, where those out for a leisurely stroll might take a break. Shortly after the bench, the trail flattens, then comes to a junction. Bear left at the junction on the dirt road, rather than the grass one, following the yellow arrow. The trail meets another junction at about 0.4 mile. Bear left, continuing uphill.

By 0.5 mile, the trail crosses a muddy area before meeting a third junction. Bear left, climbing past another bench. The trail levels off, traversing a small glade of tall softwoods. It crests a knoll, then descends slightly to a picnic table near the edge of Kilburn Crag at 0.7 mile.

Kilburn Crag gives a big view for a little hike. Littleton lies below. Mount Washington and the entire Presidential Range make up the left (east) side of the panorama. The pointed peak of Mount Garfield and the slides on the west face of Mount Lafayette are ahead, and the ski trails on Cannon Mountain lie to the right (south).

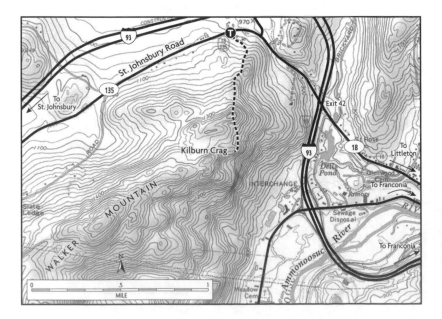

Jane at Kilburn Crags above Littleton

16. Mount Lafayette

Total distance: 8.8 miles
Hiking time: 6.5 hours
High point: 5260 feet
Elevation gain: 3300 feet
Difficulty: 4 paws (strenuous)
Map: USGS Franconia Quad B
Location: Franconia Notch State Park; Franconia, NH
Contact: Appalachian Mountain Club (AMC), 603-466-2721,
   www.outdoors.org; White Mountain National Forest–Pemigewasset/
   Ammonoosuc District, 603-869-2626, *www.fs.fed.us/r9/white;*
   Franconia Notch State Park, 603-271-3254, *www.nhstateparks.org*

Getting there, Skookumchuck trailhead (end of hike): Look for the parking lot on the east side of Route 3, just north of Route 3's split with Interstate 93. The parking lot is also the northern end of the Franconia Notch bike path. Leave one car here.

To Greenleaf trailhead (recommended start): From Interstate 93, take Exit 34B for the Cannon Mountain Tramway. Park in the tramway lot closest to the highway. The trailhead is on the opposite side of the interstate. Walk under the overpass and turn left. The trailhead is on your right.

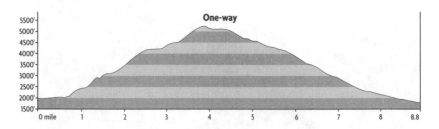

Named for the French soldier and Revolutionary War hero, the Marquis de Lafayette, Mount Lafayette is the crown jewel of Franconia Ridge and the highest peak outside the Presidential Range. It is the sixth highest mountain in the White Mountains, but perhaps the most magnificent for hiking.

There are several approaches to Lafayette. The classic route crosses the dramatic ridgeline between Mounts Lincoln and Lafayette via the Falling Waters Trail and Old Bridle Path Trail. However, if Mount Lafayette is your goal and if you are willing to drop a car a mere five minutes from your starting point, the Greenleaf Trail (blue blazes) is an uncrowded, direct route to the summit, and the Skookumchuck Trail (blue blazes) is the most paw-friendly way down. The combination also offers the most varied combination of terrain and scenery, including cascading water and a long ridge-walk.

Be sure to put a leash on your dog for the short walk from the Cannon Tramway parking lot to the trailhead. The rock-strewn Greenleaf Trail runs parallel to the highway for a half mile before crossing a small stream and veering upward. The trail squeezes between two boulders as you quickly gain altitude. Soon the Cannon Cliffs appear through the trees to the right (south).

At 1.5 miles, the trail levels off briefly through the bottom of Eagle Pass. A sheer cliff rises to your left. You are about to go up the steep ridge to the right. Step along the large rocks to the right of a small cave, gradually ascending as you traverse the pass. The trail gets rougher and more eroded as it gets steeper, soon becoming a heart-pounder. Carry plenty of water and allow frequent water breaks for your dog, particularly if he starts to lag or his chin looks foamy. There is no reliable water or even mud in which to cool off your dog until you reach Eagle Lake beyond the AMC's Greenleaf Hut.

The trail finally levels off through a low spruce corridor just before reaching the Greenleaf Hut at 2.7 miles, where the Old Bridle Path Trail converges with the Greenleaf Trail. You should put your dog on a leash as you approach the hut, as there are usually many hikers hanging out there. (Dogs are not allowed inside AMC huts.) The Greenleaf Trail and the Greenleaf Hut are not named for the predominant flora, which is decidedly not leafy, but for Colonel C. H. Greenleaf, a proprietor of the Profile House in Franconia Notch in the 1800s. Cut in 1826, the Greenleaf Trail is the oldest route up Mount Lafayette. Its namesake AMC hut was built in 1929.

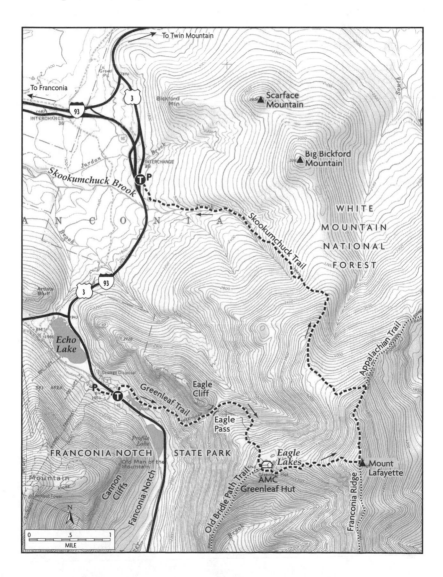

From the Greenleaf Hut it is over a mile and another 1050 vertical feet to the summit. The "peak" that you see from the hut is merely a prominent bluff. The trail passes to the right side of the hut, then dips down, crossing a small stream that flows into Eagle Lake immediately on your left. Try to prevent your dog from treading on the re-vegetation area between the trail and the small lake. Cool him off in the stream.

From the lake, the trail ascends through scrubby spruce, breaking through tree line at 3.2 miles. From this point, you are in a fragile alpine zone. Please keep yourself and your dog on the trail, which is outlined through the scree and follows a series of large rock cairns. This area is also extremely exposed, so it is best to avoid it in high winds and bad weather, particularly if there is a threat of thunderstorms. The climb is persistent, but so is the view, particularly back toward the hut and Cannon Cliffs.

The views from the summit are even more glorious. Franconia Ridge extends north and south. Over the back (west) side of the summit, you can gaze across the Pemigewasset Wilderness to the Presidential Range. On a clear day you can see smoke from the cog railway as it travels up the left side of Mount Washington. To the east, Lonesome Lake is nestled in a cirque surrounded by the Kinsmans (left) and Cannon Mountain. Echo Lake lies below the ski trails. Mount Moosilauke rises beyond, with the Green Mountains of Vermont in the far distance.

The stone foundation is all that remains of the Mount Lafayette Summit House, which was built in 1855. The Summit House lasted only ten years, but its rock foundation still offers a modicum of shelter on a breezy day.

From the summit, turn north (left) on the Garfield Ridge Trail, which is also the Appalachian Trail (white blazes), and walk across the skyline 0.7 mile to the intersection with the Skookumchuck Trail. On the last large hump of the ridge, turn left on the Skookumchuck Trail, toward the highway, which lies like two white ribbons in the valley below. The sign may be missing, but it is the first intersection after leaving the summit. The trail immediately enters a fir forest, becoming noticeably softer and less rocky underfoot. A carpet of wood sorrel, moss, and ferns spreads out from the trail.

About 2 miles from the summit, the trail starts to follow a small stream, which eventually grows into Skookumchuck Brook. There are many small pools next to the trail, perfect for cooling off your dog and soaking your tired feet.

At 3 miles from the summit, the trail gets steeper briefly as it descends

Opposite: Franconia Ridge between Mount Lafayette and Mount Garfield

over a hundred stone steps through a temperate rain forest. The foliage is lush, and the air is noticeably more humid. Green moss covers the rocks in the brook. There are more stepping stones across a small mud flat, where two more streams tumble into the Skookumchuck Brook.

At 3.9 miles from the summit, the trail goes up over a rise as it bends away from the brook. You can hear car sounds, but you are not close to the trailhead yet. The trail meanders through a hardwood forest for a long 1.1 miles as it parallels the road. After the second intersection with the Heritage Trail, a multi-use trail that is mainly used for snowmobiling, put your dog on his leash. The parking lot is finally just ahead.

The Skookumchuck Trail is probably the least-used route on Mount Lafayette because it is a full 5 miles from the top to the trailhead, but it takes about the same amount of time to descend it as it does to go up the Greenleaf Trail.

17. The Moats

Total distance: 9.6 miles
Hiking time: 7.5 hours
High point: 3201 feet (North Moat); 2802 feet (Middle Moat); 2772 feet (South Moat)
Elevation gain: 3300 feet
Difficulty: 4 paws (strenuous)
Fees and permits: $3 day fee (parking fee) at Diana's Baths trailhead
Pet policy: Dogs should be leashed until past Diana's Baths
Maps: USGS North Conway West Quad; USGS Silver Lake Quad
Location: North Conway, NH
Contact: White Mountain National Forest–Saco District, 603-447-5448, *www.fs.fed.us/r9/white*

Getting there, Passaconaway Road trailhead (end of hike): From the Kancamagus Highway (Route 112), turn into the Albany Covered Bridge Campground on Passaconaway Road (also called the Dugway). Bear right off the covered bridge, continuing on Passaconaway Road for about 4 miles. The trailhead for South Moat is on the left by the brown sign with the hiker symbol, at the entrance to Hammond Lane. There is no parking area; best parking is on the shoulder of the road. Leave one car here.

To Diana's Baths trailhead on West Side Road (recommended start):

From Passaconaway Road, turn left on Allens Siding Road. At the T, turn left onto West Side Road. Turn left two more times, staying on West Side Road. Park at the trailhead for Diana's Baths.

The Moats make up a long ridge that runs along the west side of North Conway, paralleling the Saco River. There are three Moat peaks—North, Middle, and South. North is the highest at 3201 feet. The ridge-walk from Moat to Moat is one of the finest in New England. Much of it is bare due to a forest fire many years ago, and the views are marvelous.

Some people prefer to hike a loop that begins at Diana's Baths, climbs North Moat via the Moat Mountain Trail (yellow blazes), then descends via the Red Ridge Trail back to Diana's Baths. The hike across the whole ridge is about the same mileage. It requires a car drop, but rewards with sustained views, and three summits instead of one. The route described here is the Moat Range from north to south, preferable because you escape the crowds at Diana's Baths early. Also North Moat, the first peak you reach, is almost at the halfway point, which makes the hike out from South Moat seem fairly short.

From a dog's perspective, the first couple of miles are nirvana, along some of the best swimming holes in the region. The upper part of the ridge is typically dry, and there are a couple of steep, ledgy areas, but nothing insurmountable for a mountain-savvy canine.

Diana's Baths are actually pools formed by Lucy Brook as it tumbles down a lower shoulder of North Moat. The trail follows the north bank of Lucy Brook past an old dam, then bears right away from the cascades along a smaller stream for a few paces, turns left up a hill, and returns to Lucy Brook.

After a gentle climb along the brook, the trail flattens on a traverse. At 1.3 miles, the trail crosses a smaller tributary of Lucy Brook on a primitive log bridge, then comes to a junction with the Red Ridge Trail. If you hike the loop, rather than the entire ridge, you will come out here. Continue straight (right) on the Moat Mountain Trail, keeping Lucy Brook on your left.

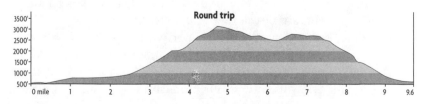

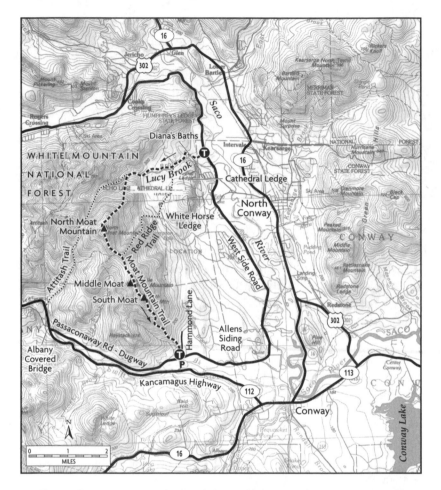

The trail continues on the level through the woods, veering away from Lucy Brook. It is wide and smooth. At 1.5 miles, it arcs back to the brook, then turns left to cross over it on rocks. Dog paws will certainly get wet here regardless of the conditions, and human feet could get damp here too, if the water is high.

After a few more stream crossings, the trail returns to the south side of Lucy Brook, hemmed in by a hillside on the left. There are several more pools, fed by lovely cascades along this stretch of the brook.

At 2.5 miles, the trail reaches the junction with the Attitash Trail. The Moat Mountain Trail turns left (south), uphill, leaving Lucy Brook for good but following a smaller tributary on the left. The trail immediately becomes less forgiving. It ascends stiffly through an open hemlock glade.

By 2.9 miles, after gaining noticeable altitude, the trees shrink and the soil gives way more frequently to rock.

At 3.7 miles the grade moderates, then the trail opens up onto an expanse of slab where you will find the first good views to the east, of Kearsarge North with its fire tower and Black Cap where the Cranmore Mountain Resort is located. Stay on the right side of the slab to remain on the trail. At 4.1 miles and the next flat area, North Moat's summit cone comes into view just before you head into some taller softwoods.

Moat Mountain Trail between Middle Moat and South Moat

The final effort up North Moat is steep and rough, over coarse rubble at first. It is a direct, sustained climb, but less than a half mile. At 4.5 miles the trail turns back to slab and reaches the summit of North Moat. The panorama is BIG, with Mount Washington anchoring the Presidential Range to the north. The ridge to South Moat lies before you to the south, not to be confused with Red Ridge, the cliff that forms the wall with the valley below. The Moat ridge is slightly west and less obvious from this lookout. Conway Lake lies to the east of the Moats. Ossipee Lake, Silver Lake, and Mount Chocorua are southwest of the ridge. The rocky top due west is Mount Osceola.

Head straight over the summit of North Moat, reentering the woods. There is a short, steep scramble down some ledge, easier for dogs than humans. From there, the trail hugs a tall rock, then drops down two more vertical sections before a more normal descent through softwoods.

After a short climb up another ledge, the trail descends a 10-foot rock "face" requiring an easy friction climb by humans. Again, dogs seem to have no problem if given the freedom to pick their route.

At 5.5 miles the trail climbs to a knoll where the Red Ridge Trail exits left amid an acre of blueberry bushes. Continue straight to keep the ridge, then take the left spur through a split in a boulder for another excellent view to the east. South Moat looms closer to the south.

The main trail bends right, descending again until it enters more softwoods on noticeably softer, flatter terrain. As the trail approaches Middle Moat, it begins to climb again and becomes a mosaic of roots, which soon give way to familiar slab. The route bears right across the first clearing, then left through scrub trees.

At 6.5 miles the trail passes the summit of Middle Moat, continuing on open rock most of the way toward South Moat. Watch the blazes carefully in this area. The trail is poorly marked, but if you keep to the obvious ridgeline you will be fine. After cresting a rocky knoll, the trail bends right, downhill, and the rock peters out. It traverses a col, then climbs on open slab, with constant views east and west as the ridge narrows. At 7.2 miles it reaches South Moat and another dramatic 360-degree view.

The view to Ossipee Lake and Silver Lake remain during the upper portion of the descent, which goes a long way over slab, even after the view is obscured by woods. At the bottom of the bedrock, the trail steepens and turns to loose rubble. The footing is crumbly and uncertain, but only for a short way. Then the trail levels off and smooths out, passing through an airy forest. Just after the forest becomes deciduous, the trail turns into a logging road. Continue straight ahead, ignoring the other logging roads that crisscross the area.

At 9.6 miles the trail bends right, merging with a dirt road. A chain-link fence blocks the route straight ahead into a field. This dirt road is Hammond Lane, which meets Passaconaway Road after about 200 yards.

18. Mount Monroe

Round trip: 10 miles
Hiking time: 7 hours
High point: 5384 feet
Elevation gain: 3354 feet
Difficulty: 4 paws (strenuous)
Fees and permits: $3 parking fee (day-use fee) at the trailhead
Pet policy: None, but to preserve fragile alpine plants, please leash dogs above tree line
Maps: USGS Crawford Notch Quad; USGS Stairs Mtn Quad; USGS Mount Washington Quad
Location: Crawford Notch, NH
Contact: Appalachian Mountain Club (AMC), 603-466-2721, *www.outdoors.org;* White Mountain National Forest–Androscoggin District, 603-466-2713, *www.fs.fed.us/r9/white*

Getting there: From Route 302 in Crawford Notch, turn onto the Mount Clinton Road. (Note: The sign is only visible heading toward Bretton Woods. If approaching from Bretton Woods, turn at the sign for the Crawford Path trailhead.) The trailhead to Mount Monroe via the Edmands Path is just over 2 miles from Route 302 on the right.

Named for the fifth president of the United States, Mount Monroe gets only a fraction of the attention lavished on its neighbor, Mount Washington,

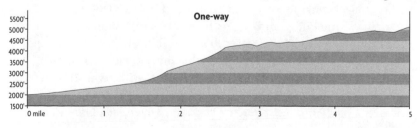

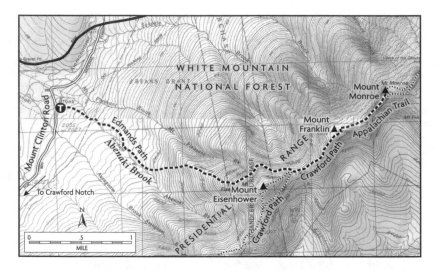

but it merits much more. Monroe is the fourth highest peak in New Hampshire and the highest of the southern Presidential Range.

The approach to Mount Monroe from the Edmands Path (blue blazes) is also a common approach to Mount Eisenhower. Eisenhower is an impressive open dome and a shorter hike, both in terms of mileage (6.8 miles round trip) and vertical gain (2730 feet), which also tends to make it more crowded. If you and your dog have the time and the stamina, the hike to Monroe crosses one of the most dramatic ridges in the Northeast.

The Edmands Path is an historic trail that goes from Mount Clinton Road to the middle of the Crawford Path, between Mount Eisenhower and Mount Franklin. The trail is named for J. Raynor Edmands, who constructed the trail in 1909. To this day, it is considered one of the most well-constructed trails in the White Mountains, climbing at a relatively even pitch despite the rugged terrain.

The path is smooth and flat at first, crossing two small streams on log footbridges within the first ten minutes. At 0.4 mile it crosses the more substantial Abenaki Brook on a constructed bridge. The trail bends to the right off the bridge and begins to climb gently, angling away from the brook. The path widens, resembling an old, slightly eroded logging road, and at 0.7 mile begins to climb steadily. As you gain altitude, the trees become predominantly birch and spruce, with ferns underneath.

Opposite: Mount Washington framed by Mount Monroe and Little Monroe

The train whistle in the distance is the cog railway chugging up Mount Washington a few miles to the north across Ammonoosuc Ravine.

At 2.2 miles the trail passes through a switchback to the left, then across stone steps to a cut in a man-made stone wall. The valley floor is now far below. The trail hugs the side of the mountain, hanging like a long, narrow terrace as it angles upward. Through openings in the trees, you can see the red roof of the Mount Washington Hotel below to the left, and Mount Washington itself above to the right.

At 2.5 miles a small cascade tumbles down a rocky wall, turning into a stream that crosses the trail. This is a great place take a break with your dog. From here it is a scramble up rocks past another small cascade, the last chance for water. Use caution after a rainstorm, as the path itself becomes a stream.

A few minutes later the trail finally levels off, traversing in a northeasterly direction. The view to the left is a continual panorama from Mount Franklin past Mounts Monroe, Washington, Clay, and Jefferson. At 2.8 miles the trail leaves the trees. Despite the extremely difficult growing conditions, it is remarkable how many hues of green spread around you—rare lichens, wildflowers, berries, and grasses coat much of the rock.

At 3 miles, just after crossing a short bit of scree, the Edmands Path ends at the Crawford Path/Appalachian Trail (white blazes) in the col between Eisenhower and Franklin. Turn left (east) to begin the traverse of the ridge. The trail passes just below the summit of Mount Franklin. Although Mount Franklin is a lofty 5004 feet, it is not considered a 4000-footer in its own right due its close proximity to Mount Monroe. In fact, its summit is a rather indistinct hump on the shoulder of Monroe from this angle.

At 4.5 miles, turn left onto the Monroe loop, which goes over Little Monroe and the main summit. As you approach, Mount Washington is framed between the two Monroe peaks. This is a place for surefooted dogs, requiring a short stretch of boulder-hopping near both pinnacles. (Note: The area within the Monroe loop is extremely fragile and of great botanical importance. Please keep Fido under control and on the trail.)

At 4.9 miles the trail reaches the summit of Mount Monroe. The view is mind-boggling on a clear day. The Davis Path runs along the ridge to the east. Look down into Oakes Gulf on one side, then across to Mount Washington and the northern Presidential Range on the other. To the west, the highest ridge on the horizon is Franconia Ridge.

19. Mount Osceola

Round trip: 6.4 miles
Hiking time: 4.5 hours
High point: 4340 feet
Elevation gain: 2050 feet
Difficulty: 3 paws (ambitious)
Fees and permits: $3 day-use (parking) fee
Map: USGS Mount Osceola Quad
Location: Waterville Valley, NH
Contact: White Mountain National Forest–White Mountain
Gateway Visitor Center, 603-745-3816, *www.fs.fed.us/r9/white*

Getting there: Take Route 49 to Waterville Valley. Turn left on Tripoli Road, heading toward the ski area. At the fork, just below the ski area, bear right, continuing on Tripoli Road over Thornton Gap. The trailhead is on the right about 5 miles from the fork. (Note: The Tripoli Road past the ski area is closed during the winter.)

Mount Osceola is named for the legendary Seminole chief who waged war against U.S. troops during the late 1830s when the government tried to move his people from Florida to Oklahoma. He died in prison in 1837. He never visited his namesake peak in New Hampshire. In fact, it was likely not named for him until late in the nineteenth century. The reason is unknown. A map of the region, circa 1860, refers to it as "Mad River Peak."

Mount Osceola is the highest mountain in the Waterville Valley area, dominating the northwestern end of the valley. There are two approaches to the summit, one from Tripoli Road in Thornton Gap and the other via the Greeley Pond Trail and East Osceola, a 4000-footer in its own right. The Greeley Ponds are a high-use area. In addition, there is a "chimney," a non-technical vertical climb between the lower, tree-covered East Peak and

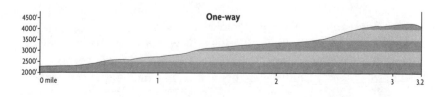

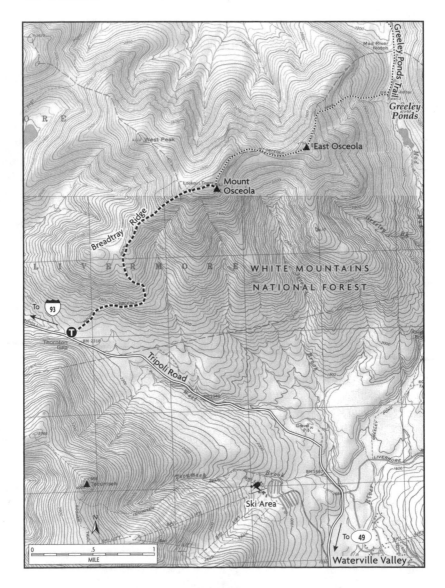

the main summit of Osceola, making this route doubly un-dog-friendly. If the main peak of Osceola is your goal, the approach from the Tripoli Road is more direct and definitely preferable with a dog.

The trail is relatively flat as it enters the woods with uneven footing resembling a dry streambed. Within five minutes, the trail crosses a real stream, dips briefly, then heads upward. It is a moderately steep trail,

made challenging more by the uneven footing than the grade. After
bending sharply to the left, the trail crosses a trickle from a spring and
a short section of slab before entering a corridor where birch trees line
up like white sentinels along green spruce walls. The trail continues to
be eroded and wide.

At 1.3 miles, several switchbacks lead up to Breadtray Ridge. The trail
levels off on the ridge and the footing becomes much smoother, as you
traverse in a northeasterly direction toward the summit.

After crossing a length of wet slab that turns into a cliff farther into
the woods to your right, the trail bends left, climbing over a short
four-foot ledge. Most dogs have little problem here, but a small dog
may need to be spotted. Glance right through the trees for a view of
Mount Tecumseh. About ten minutes later, the canopy dissolves as you
head over a long stretch of side-hill slab, then up several switchbacks.
At the next level section, you can see Franconia Ridge through the low
spruce trees.

East Osceola from the summit cliffs on Mount Osceola

Shortly after crossing a flat, muddy area, the trail passes the anchors for the former fire tower. Put your dog on his leash here, as the summit cliff is directly ahead. The summit is a wide perch with a truly incredible view. Mount Washington and the Presidential Range are to the north. Mount Tripyramid with its obvious slide is nearby to the east. The big rocky peak in the distance behind Tripyramid is Mount Chocorua. Waterville Valley lies below, with Squam Lake separated by a ridge to the south.

20. Mount Pemigewasset (Indian Head)

Round trip: 3.6 miles
Hiking time: 3 hours
High point: 2557 feet
Elevation gain: 1157 feet
Difficulty: 2 paws (moderate)
Map: USGS Lincoln Quad
Location: Franconia Notch State Park; between Franconia and North Woodstock, NH
Contact: New Hampshire Division of Parks and Recreation, 603-271-3556, *www.nhstateparks.org*

Getting there: Take Route 3 or Interstate 93 into Franconia Notch State Park. Exit at The Flume Visitor Center. Best parking is in the northernmost lot at the visitor center.

Mount Pemigewasset is also called Indian Head because the mountain is shaped like the profile of a Native American. There are two trails up Mount Pemigewasset, the Indian Head Trail and the Mount Pemigewasset Trail. About the same length, they converge just below the summit. The

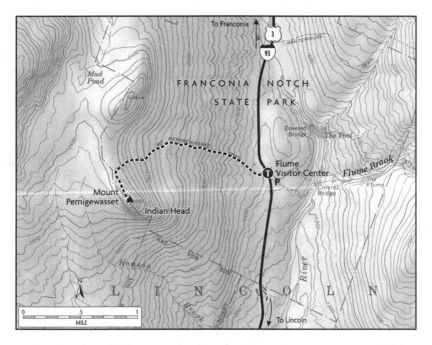

Indian Head Trail is less popular, but the Mount Pemigewasset Trail (blue blazes) is preferable because it has easy parking and nearby bathroom facilities at The Flume Visitor Center. Not that the Mount Pemigewasset Trail is overcrowded. The Flume, a narrow gorge with man-made walkways, is accessible from the back of the visitor center for a small fee. It draws most of the tourist traffic, leaving Mount Pemigewasset surprisingly quiet, despite the moderate mileage and the breathtaking views from its summit.

With its easy footing and modest mileage and elevation gain, the Mount Pemigewasset Trail is a perfect hike for an older dog, a small dog, or a large puppy. From the parking lot, walk north on the bike path for 150 yards to the trailhead, which leaves the bike path to the left and passes quickly through three tunnels. The first tunnel takes you immediately under Route 3. The other two tunnels take you under the northbound and southbound lanes of Interstate 93. After the last tunnel the trail begins to head upward, soon crossing a stream.

The next water crossing is about halfway to the top. Let your dog take advantage of this one. After this point, the trail veers away from the stream. The trail continues to ascend at a moderate rate. You know you are almost there when the trees turn to hemlock and the trail begins to

Jane gets a hug on the summit of Mount Pemigewasset.

get easier. A view southwest toward the Kinsman Range is merely a sneak preview of what lies ahead.

A few moments later, the trail breaks onto the open, rocky top. On a clear day, the views are staggering, with Mount Moosilauke to the southwest (right) through the Lost River Gap. Interstate 93 cuts through the valley far below, like two ribbons heading to the horizon. The ski trails on Loon Mountain are visible to the southeast (left) at the head of another valley that ends with square-topped Mount Osceola in the distance.

Take care at the top of the mountain. While the open, rocky area is sizable, the cliff straight ahead is obvious and sheer. This is a good place to keep your dog on a short lead and on level rock if she is inclined to wander. The footing on the sloping portion of the rock can be slippery when wet.

The view becomes even more spectacular if you walk down the rock to the left, where the entire Franconia Ridge looms before you.

21. Mounts Pierce and Eisenhower

Round trip: 9.6 miles
Hiking time: 7 hours
High points: 4312 feet (Mount Pierce); 4760 feet (Mount Eisenhower)
Elevation gain: 3200 feet
Difficulty: 4 paws (strenuous)
Fees and permits: $3 day-use (parking) fee
Pet policy: Pets should be kept on trail above tree line to protect fragile alpine plants
Maps: USGS Stairs Mountain Quad; USGS Crawford Notch Quad
Location: Crawford Notch, NH
Contact: Appalachian Mountain Club (AMC), 603-466-2721, *www.outdoors.org*; White Mountain National Forest–Androscoggin District, 603-466-2713, *www.fs.fed.us/r9/white*

Getting there: On Route 302, just west of the top of Crawford Notch, turn onto Mount Clinton Road. The parking area and trailhead for the Crawford Connector are on the left. (Note: There is no parking at the official start of the Crawford Path on Route 302.)

Mount Pierce is also frequently called Mount Clinton. The name Clinton is not in honor of former President Bill Clinton, but for Dewitt Clinton (1769–1828), a governor and senator from New York. The mountain was officially renamed Mount Pierce in 1913 by the New Hampshire State Legislature in honor of Franklin Pierce, the only president of the United States from New Hampshire, but it took another seventy years before the Appalachian Mountain Club's trail maps recognized the new name. Some mapmakers continue to use the name "Clinton" or note it in parentheses, which adds to the ongoing confusion.

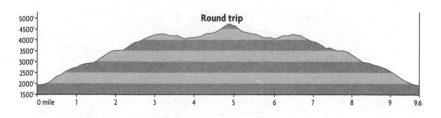

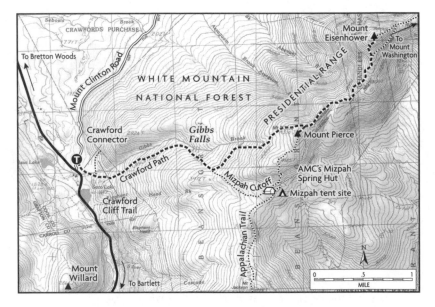

Mount Pierce is ranked twenty-seventh among the forty-eight 4000-footers in New Hampshire. It is an excellent inaugural "Presidential" hike for both people and dogs. The footing is relatively good the whole way (no boulder-hopping). Its summit offers a spectacular view of the Presidential Range to the north. Although in the alpine zone, it is less exposed.

The Crawford Path is the shortest route to the summit of Mount Pierce. Built in 1819 by Abel Crawford and his son Ethan Allen Crawford, it is the oldest continually-maintained hiking trail in the United States. During the nineteenth century it was used as a bridle path. Although it is eroded to rock in many spots today, it remains wide and has a reasonable grade, making it perfect for dogs.

The Crawford Path starts in Crawford Notch and ends atop Mount Washington, crossing the high ridge from the shoulder of Pierce, and traveling past Eisenhower, Franklin, and Monroe en route. Though it does not climb to the summit of any peak except Mount Washington, each peak has a spur trail or summit loop to accomplish that goal.

There are shorter routes to the summit of Eisenhower, but once atop Pierce it is an easy 1.6-mile ridge-walk, with dramatic views most of the way, so definitely worth the effort. Eisenhower is a landmark dome, visible from many viewpoints in the White Mountains. People often remark how appropriate that the mountain and the man are/were both bald.

From the parking area, take the Crawford Connector to the Crawford Path. The Crawford Connector crosses the Mount Clinton Road, then climbs moderately through softwoods. It is a wide, obvious trail. Stepping stones, a footbridge, and split-log bridge help hikers cross the muddier sections, although dogs tend to walk or wade through the wet areas.

At 0.3 mile, the Crawford Connector passes the Crawford Cliff Trail just before it crosses a bridge over Gibbs Brook. There are several enticing pools under the bridge in which your dog will want to play, but save it for the descent. You still have a big climb ahead.

On the opposite side of the bridge, the Crawford Connector comes to a T at the Crawford Path. Turn left by a large sign for the AMC's Mizpah Spring Hut, heading uphill. The rock-strewn trail climbs steadily, paralleling the brook. It passes an old dam, then at 0.6 mile passes a short spur to Gibbs Falls.

Gibbs Falls is named after Joseph Gibbs, a landlord of the historic Crawford House that was located near the base of the Crawford Path until 1977 when it was destroyed by fire. The narrow cascade falls into a sizable pool, which your dog will love to wade in. Again, save it for the way down.

The trail above Gibbs Falls continues to climb steadily, gradually veering away from the brook. It ascends through an old-growth forest, filled with red spruce and yellow birch. During fall foliage, the entire trail has a golden glow when the sun filters through the birch leaves. The trail crosses numerous water bars and streamlets. It is definitely well-worn, like hiking on giant cobblestones.

At about 1 mile there is a rock just beyond a streamlet in the middle of the trail, hewn by nature into the shape of a chair. Five minutes later, the grade eases a little as the path crosses a log bridge. But from there it rises steeply, with just enough flat or smooth sections to keep your pulse under 200 beats per minute.

At 1.5 miles the Crawford Path comes to a fork with the Mizpah Cutoff, the trail to the AMC's Mizpah Spring Hut and tent site. Dogs are not allowed inside AMC huts, but it is okay to tent-camp with a dog. Bear left at the fork, the flatter route, to stay on the Crawford Path.

As the trail traverses east over sections of slab, the hill rolls away to the left, skirting a height of land. For a moment there are glimpses of Mount Deception and Mount Dartmouth across the valley before the trail becomes more wooded and the rate of ascent increases.

At about 2 miles the trail crosses a length of side-hill slab. The trees

become lower (about 10 feet high) and scrawnier. The route traverses a number of logs in a wet area, then enters the alpine zone. A moment later there is an impressive view of Mount Jefferson, then in another few moments a huge vista lies before you—the main ridge of the northern Presidential Range, with Mount Eisenhower in the foreground.

At 3.1 miles the Crawford Path comes to a junction with the Webster Cliff Trail/Appalachian Trail (white blazes). Bear right onto the Webster Cliff Trail. After a short uphill burst, the path reaches the summit of Mount Pierce at 3.2 miles, marked by a large cairn, a benchmark, and a stake. Scrub trees obscure the view to the south, but it hardly matters. The crown jewel of views lies clearly to the north, toward Mount Washington.

From the summit of Mount Pierce, you can simply retrace your steps back to the car or continue to Mount Eisenhower. In both cases, descend the short distance back to the junction with the Crawford Path. To continue, turn right at the junction, heading toward the distinctive bald dome of Mount Eisenhower. The Crawford Path is now also the Appalachian Trail North.

The section of trail to Mount Eisenhower is a ridge-walk in and out of low trees, with many views of Mount Washington and Mount Eisenhower ahead, and down into Bretton Woods to the left (northeast).

At 4 miles the trail reaches a muddy col between Pierce and Eisenhower, then climbs onto an upper shoulder of the latter. Follow the rock cairns carefully, stick to bedrock, and do not allow your dog to wander on or dig in the fragile alpine vegetation that lies in patches around you.

At 4.4 miles the Crawford Path comes to a junction with the Mount Eisenhower Loop Trail, which leads over the summit. Bear left on the loop trail. It climbs steadily, reaching the summit at 4.8 miles. The broad, open top is marked by an extremely large cairn inside a ring of stones. An odd metal square protrudes from the top of the cairn, which looks like a weathered sign now reduced to its base metal.

The summit of Mount Eisenhower has one of the finest views in New England. The high Presidential Range is dramatic from this proximity and altitude. You can also see Mount Chocorua to the east, the hump of Mount Pierce and the southern Presidential Range to the south, and Bretton Woods to the southwest.

Opposite: Gibbs Falls

22. North Sugarloaf and Middle Sugarloaf

Round trip: 3.2 miles
Hiking time: 2.5 hours
High points: 2539 feet (Middle Sugarloaf); 2310 feet (North Sugarloaf)
Elevation gain: 900 feet
Difficulty: 2 paws (moderate)
Fees and permits: $3 day-use (parking) fee
Map: USGS Bethlehem Quad
Location: Twin Mountain, NH
Contact: White Mountain National Forest–White Mountain
Gateway Visitor Center, 603-745-3816, *www.fs.fed.us/r9/white/*

Getting there: From Twin Mountain, take Route 302 east. Turn right onto Zealand Road and go just past the Sugarloaf Campgrounds. The best parking is in the small day-use lot by the trailhead sign near the Zealand River. Cross over the bridge on foot and turn right to find the Sugarloaf Trail on the opposite side of the river. (Note: The "XC" (cross-country ski) trail at the parking lot is not the right trail.)

There are at least eight Sugarloaf Mountains in New Hampshire, likely named because they are fairly low in elevation and support abundant maple trees, and thus maple syrup. Three of the Sugarloaves are by Twin Mountain, but only North Sugarloaf and Middle Sugarloaf have trails. They are also the most obvious, in plain view where Route 302 crosses Route 3. Both have open tops, with excellent views, particularly into the Pemigewasset Wilderness, and for relatively little effort.

The route to the Sugarloaves is shaped like a T, with the middle peak and the north peak at each end of the crossbar. It starts along the west bank of the Zealand River. At 0.2 miles it meets the Trestle Trail, which continues along the river. The Sugarloaf Trail veers left, leaving the river

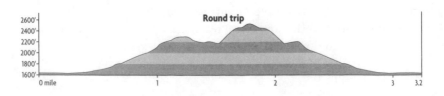

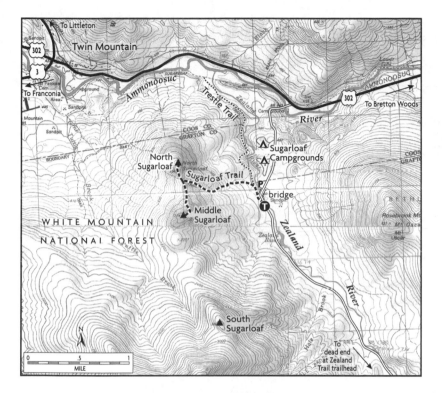

behind, and begins to climb. Moments later it crosses a grassy road, then levels off, crossing a muddy area over logs and stones as it approaches the two mountains.

The climb is gentle at first, through a pine glade. A few moments later it goes around an impressive boulder, pieces of which have split off to each side. There are a number of boulders, known as glacial erratics, along this section of trail. At 0.7 mile, the trail climbs more earnestly up a long rock staircase, through a switchback, then up more steps. At the top of this steeper section, at 0.9 mile, the trail comes to a T at the saddle between the north and middle peak.

To reach North Sugarloaf, turn right over smooth, flat slab. The trail dips quickly then descends at a more sustained rate. It passes through a rocky section before heading uphill again, climbing at an angle. After traversing around a rocky outcropping, the trail bends sharply to the right. It becomes crisscrossed with pine tree roots, then levels off again, breaking from the trees onto the summit ledges at 1.2 miles. Put your dog on a leash around this first cliff, which is narrow and seems more sheer

Hank takes his own route up the rock, avoiding the stairs on Middle Sugarloaf.

than the area to the right. The panorama includes Bretton Woods to the far left (east), the Willey Range and Mount Hale to the south, and the Twin Range to the southwest. Middle and South Sugarloaf are to the far right and much closer than the other peaks. An even better spot (good for a picnic) is farther to the right, offering a broader vista to the west and a bigger, more open, flat area on which to rest.

Continuing on, retrace your steps south, returning to the T at 1.5 miles. To reach Middle Sugarloaf, head straight, across the saddle. The trail passes over slab, then heads down through a small sag before climbing through a short steep section. The trail is scattered with rocks, but soon flattens. A few minutes later it bends to the right and goes up again, over several stretches of slab. The trail becomes noticeably more eroded just before reaching a wooden staircase. Your dog may wish to ascend by the side of the staircase, but she will have to be rather agile to make it, as the bare rock is steep and slippery. If she can climb the stairs at home, she should have no trouble here once she realizes that the wooden structure is a staircase.

The staircase empties onto another broad, rocky outcropping at 1.9 miles. The view from Middle Sugarloaf gives a different angle on the Twin Range and the Pemigewasset Wilderness. It seems more wild from this vantage point, perhaps because the road is much less conspicuous or perhaps because the final approach is more challenging.

Retrace again, heading back toward the T and returning to the car at 3.2 miles.

23. Mount Washington

Round trip: Approximately 11.5 miles (including summit)
Hiking time: 8.5 hours
High point: 6288 feet
Elevation gain: 4400 feet
Difficulty: 4+ paws (very difficult)
Pet policy: Pets should be leashed around the AMC Visitor Center
    at Pinkham Notch and around the summit area. Dogs are not
    allowed overnight at Hermit Lake Shelters.
Maps: USGS Stairs Mountain Quad; USGS Mount Washington Quad
Location: South of Gorham, NH at Pinkham Notch
Contact: Appalachian Mountain Club (AMC), 603-466-2721,
    www.outdoors.org; White Mountain National Forest–Androscoggin
    District, 603-466-2713, *www.fs.fed.us/r9/white*

Getting there: Take Route 16 to the AMC Visitor Center at Pinkham
Notch, between Glen and Gorham. Best parking is in the overflow lot,
south of the main parking lot. The trailhead is at the north end of the
overflow lot.

Mount Washington is the centerpiece of the Presidential Range and
the highest peak in the northeastern United States. Although the
summit can be reached by auto road and cog railway, it should not
be taken lightly as a hike. Snow could fall on any day of the year. The
highest wind speed ever recorded in the world was atop Mount Washington—231 miles per hour on April 12, 1934. And the record high
temperature on the summit is a cool 72 degrees, which means that
even when it is a steamy 85 degrees in the valley, the summit is likely
a chilly 55 degrees.

Mount Washington is a vast hulk, buttressed by many ridges and
thus surrounded by many deep ravines, including the famed Tucker-

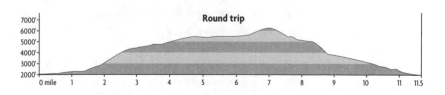

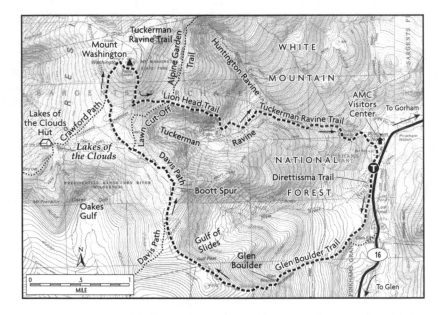

man Ravine, where backcountry skiers test their skill on its vertical slope each spring. The mountain's upper half is above tree line, which makes for dramatic hiking on a clear day but extremely difficult hiking when visibility is poor. Many people have died of exposure on this mountain. Only attempt a hike up Mount Washington on the nicest day, and be prepared for the worst.

There are a number of ways to climb Mount Washington, all long and none particularly dog-friendly. Its nickname is "The Rock Pile," because its upper slopes are a jumble of boulders. All routes pick their way through the boulder field on the top of the mountain. There are several routes that you should definitely NOT hike with a dog, particularly the extremely steep, rough trail up Huntington Ravine, where the Forest Service has performed a number of dog rescues. The Tuckerman Ravine Trail and the Great Gulf Trail are also extremely difficult for dogs because they have long, steep, rocky sections that are more vertical boulder fields than trails. Mount Washington is decidedly not one of the best hikes with a dog, but because it is the highest peak, many people wish to hike it—and bring their dogs. That said, what is the best way to bag this peak with your pet?

The easiest and one of the shortest routes, although still a lengthy 10 miles round trip, is up the Jewell Trail, which departs from the base of the cog railway, but it is also among the most crowded routes, beginning and ending at major tourist destinations, and the least pleasing because it is rather close to the cog most of the way up. A purer wilderness experience can be had on the opposite side of the mountain. Make a loop ascending by the Glen Boulder Trail to the Davis Path, then descending via the Lion Head Trail. This loop also gives you the choice of going to the summit or not. But even if you do not, you will still have a long alpine hike with some of the most breathtaking mountain views in New England.

From the AMC Visitor Center, take the Direttissma Trail (yellow blazes), paralleling Route 16 through the woods, which connects to the Glen Boulder Trail at 1 mile. Turn right, to begin the real climb.

At 1.4 miles the Avalanche Brook ski trail leaves to the left. Soon after, you begin following a rushing brook on your left. The trail crosses

View of the summit of Mount Washington from the Davis Path

the brook by a pretty cascade. There is a perfect doggie pool next to the trail just below the crossing. A little farther along, the trail bends to the right by a large boulder. From there it bends back toward the brook, then around a switchback, heading upward in a northwestern direction.

Although the Glen Boulder Trail is not as heavily used as other routes on Mount Washington, it is an old trail and rather eroded. The climb is persistent. At 2 miles it clears the trees, with a scramble up a ledge. From the ledge you can see Boott Spur on the right, the rocky outcropping that marks the southern wall of Tuckerman Ravine. Moments later the entire Wildcat Ridge appears behind you.

The approach to the Glen Boulder goes up the left side of the Gulf of Slides. It can be tricky in places, but nothing serious for an experienced mountain dog. Follow the rock cairns which mark the route better than the blazes. The Glen Boulder perches above to the left. A glacial erratic left behind by the last ice age, it seems to defy gravity, balancing in the middle of a wide, bare shoulder of the mountain. The trail reenters the scrub trees briefly, then emerges just below the boulder at 2.2 miles.

Above Glen Boulder the trail continues upward, soon allowing your first view of the summit above Tuckerman Ravine. You can hear the whistle of the cog railway as you climb steadily over ledge and rocky rubble. At 2.6 miles the trail finally flattens, traversing through some low softwoods before breaking from the tree line for good. It continues on a more moderate grade around the rim of the Gulf of Slides.

The rock-strewn trail continues to climb through a lawn of alpine grasses, wild blueberries, and lingonberries (alpine cranberries). At 4.2 miles the Glen Boulder Trail ends at the Davis Path. Turn right on the Davis Path, traversing a massive plateau past Boott Spur and along the top of Tuckerman Ravine. This is a desolate yet beautiful area, an expanse of rugged mountain terrain on a scale unequaled elsewhere in the Northeast. A hiker and a dog feel like tiny ants on the back of an impossibly large elephant here.

If you do not wish to go to the summit, turn right at 4.8 miles on the Lawn Cut-Off, circumnavigating the top of Tuckerman Ravine until the Cut-Off meets the Lion Head Trail. If the peak is your goal, continue on the Davis Path up the southeastern side of the cone. A number of trails converge with the Davis Path, which turns into a pile of rubble. This is a difficult section for both humans and dogs. Dogs should be leashed because the trail becomes quite crowded, particularly above Lakes of the Clouds, where there is a constant stream of people between the summit and the AMC hut there. Yet the trail is mainly over uneven rock, which makes it difficult to hike with your dog on a leash. The Davis Path joins the Appalachian Trail (white blazes) for the final scramble, reaching the summit a lofty 6.7 miles from the car.

The summit of Mount Washington is harsh, not only in terms of weather, but also to one's backcountry senses. It is usually crowded, with tourists milling around. There are several summit structures, including the Tip Top House (a former lodge) and the Governor Sherman Adams Building, which houses the Mount Washington Observatory, a museum, a cafeteria, rest rooms, and a gift shop. About the only good reason for going to the top with a dog is to refill your water bottles.

To complete your hike, retrace your steps down the Davis Path to the Lawn Cut-Off to reach the Lion Head Trail. Some opt to depart from the summit via the Tuckerman Ravine Trail, but this a steep boulder field, difficult for even the most mountain-savvy canines. It is doable, but not recommended.

The Lion Head Trail descends along the northern rim of Tuckerman Ravine, with awesome views into the ravine for much of the way until you pass Lion Head itself, a rocky outcropping that marks the tip of the northern wall of the ravine opposite Boott Spur. The descent to this point, around the big rocks approaching Lion Head, is more challenging for humans than for dogs. Just before Lion Head the trail crosses some scree, then enters low fir trees on a short plateau, passing a spring, the first water since the stream crossing on the Glen Boulder Trail. Then the trail passes an intersection with the Alpine Garden Trail, continuing straight to Lion Head.

After the "Head," the route becomes more trail-like, although far from smooth. It descends steeply over rocks and dirt, a rock slab and a half-buried boulder, then goes around a cliff, and finally ends at the junction with the Tuckerman Ravine Trail just below the Hermit Lake Shelters, over 2 miles below the summit.

Turn left (northeast) onto the wide, well-used Tuckerman Ravine Trail. From here, it is an easy but long 2.3 miles to Pinkham Notch. The trail crosses the substantial Ellis River in three spots. Wait for the third crossing before letting your dog soak his tired paws; it has the best pool and the easiest access. Just when you think you cannot walk another step, you will reach the Visitors Center and your car.

24. Welch Mountain–Dickey Mountain Loop

Round trip: 4.4 miles
Hiking time: 3.5 hours
High points: 2734 feet (Dickey Mountain); 2605 feet (Welch Mountain)
Elevation gain: 1830 feet
Difficulty: 3 paws (ambitious)
Fees and permits: $3 day-use (parking) fee
Map: USGS Waterville Valley Quad
Location: Campton, NH
Contact: White Mountain National Forest–White Mountain
    Gateway Visitor Center, 603-745-3816, *www.fs.fed.us/r9/white*

Getting there: Take Exit 28, "Campton/Waterville Valley," off Interstate 93. Go about 6 miles on Route 49 toward Waterville Valley. Turn left on Upper Mad River Road, then right on Orris Road. The trailhead and its substantial parking lot are 0.6 mile up on the right.

Welch Mountain and its taller brother, Dickey Mountain are about half the size of their towering 4000-foot neighbors, yet they offer one of the most exposed hikes and sustained views in this part of the Whites. Most people hike the loop going up Welch and down Dickey, which is the obvious route from the parking lot. In this direction, even if the lot looks full, you will only see those you catch or those who pass you. (Note: This hike can be treacherous if the rocks are wet.)

While a superb hike for any human who loves acres of open rock and huge panoramas, it is best reserved for larger, agile dogs. There are a couple of tricky spots on the upper elevations that require a dog to stretch up the rock, or bound off it, depending on the spot.

The well-used Welch Mountain Trail (yellow blazes) follows a substantial brook into the woods, crossing the brook over large rocks. (Dogs will wade right in, but will probably not wallow here since the

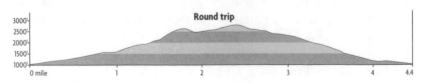

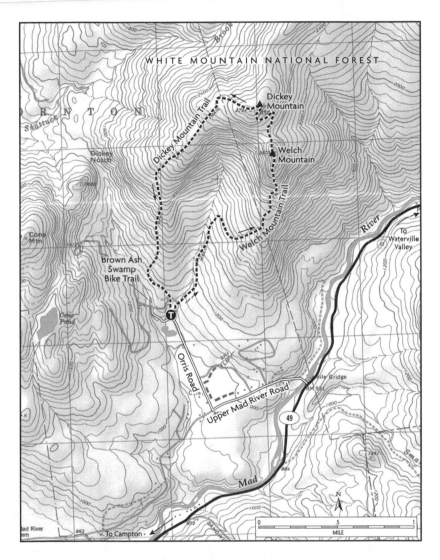

hike has barely begun.) The trail continues up the other side of the brook on easy grades. After a split-log bridge, it passes a large log hewn into a bench. At about 0.5 mile the trail bends to the right, away from the brook and climbs through an airy forest. It traverses in a southerly direction, angling upward until it reaches a short switchback, then resumes its angled climb, eventually bending left over an impressive length of shallow slab.

At 0.9 mile the trail turns right over open rock, reaching a fine perch with a view of the valley and Route 49 below. Tripyramid and the Sandwich Range form the opposite wall of the valley. Dickey Mountain is the rocky knob to the left. Wild blueberries are everywhere!

Follow the blazes closely from here. The trail weaves around shrubs and trees and over open bedrock. Soon, Tenney Mountain's ski trails appear to the southwest, with a number of other peaks now visible to the west. From here, the trail heads up over a huge expanse of granite. It is tough to continue climbing because the views are distracting, but they get even better the higher you go. There are several ledgy areas where you might have to spot your dog, though they pose little problem if you take a moment to find the best route.

The trail squeezes between two boulders, then crosses another expanse of granite as it angles to the right. What were narrow views below are now panoramas, particularly to the southwest. The view becomes a 360-degree jaw-dropper from the summit of Welch Mountain at 1.9 miles. The hulk beyond Dickey Mountain to the northwest is Mount Moosilauke. Tripyramid, which dominates the view across the valley for the entire hike, looms closer.

From the summit, the trail descends over more ledges, like natural steps, to a large cairn in the saddle between the two mountains. It enters a grove of spruce trees before heading up again, first over slab, then over roots and rocks. The trail is narrow and eroded through this area, but after a short scramble it breaks onto another expanse of bedrock just below the summit of Dickey. Welch is clearly visible behind and below you. You can also glimpse the end of Squam Lake to the south through the gap.

At 2.3 miles you reach the top of Dickey. The reward is yet another view, this time of Franconia Ridge and the Cannon Cliffs to the north. Although the summit of Dickey is not as open as the summit of Welch, the views are excellent. This is a good spot to give your dog some water and a biscuit, as most of this hike is dry.

From here, the Dickey Mountain Trail descends moderately over bedrock with wider views of the mountains to the west and northwest. At the first open expanse of rock off the summit, stay high across the top of it, then head directly down the far side for the best footing. Generally, the trail heads down a rocky ridge in a westerly direction, but as on Welch, watch the blazes and cairns carefully. The trail winds in and out of the trees and over open rock, often taking an odd turn or traversing at an unexpected angle. As you descend, look back for a view of both Welch and Dickey, twin humps covered by a patchwork of trees and granite.

Large cairn in the saddle between Welch Mountain and Dickey Mountain

Then look forward, because the trail follows the wide, flat top of a cliff before taking a sharp right into the trees.

After passing alongside a head-high ridge of rock, the trail becomes a softer forest path. The rest of the descent is well maintained on moderate to easy grades, with a number of steps built into the trail. About ten minutes after passing another log bench, it intersects with the Brown Ash Swamp Bike Trail, a woods road. Turn left to find the parking lot around the next bend.

25. Mount Willard

Round trip: 2.8 miles

Hiking time: 2 hours

High point: 2804 feet

Elevation gain: 925 feet

Difficulty: 2 paws (moderate)

Map: USGS Crawford Notch Quad

Location: Crawford Notch State Park; between Bretton Woods and Bartlett, NH

Contact: Appalachian Mountain Club (AMC), 603-466-2721, *www.outdoors.org;* White Mountain National Forest–Androscoggin District, 603-466-2713, *www.fs.fed.us/r9/white;* Crawford Notch State Park, 603-271-3254, *www.nhstateparks.org*

Getting there: Take Route 302 to Crawford Notch. The trailhead is on the south side of the road behind the AMC's Macomber Family Information Center (old train depot) on the other side of the railroad tracks. Best parking is across the road at either end of Saco Lake.

While Mount Willard is about half the size of its Presidential neighbors, it is the perfect hike if you are short on time, passing through this area of New Hampshire, and in need of a view. It is a popular hike because it is a relatively easy 1.4 miles to the top, so probably not the best choice on a clear-weather weekend if you have an antisocial dog. But midweek, the odds are better that you will have the trail to yourself.

Put a leash on your dog out of the car. Although a two-lane road, Route 302 is a major east–west corridor in New Hampshire.

Take the Avalon Trail for about 100 yards, to the intersection with the Mount Willard Trail (blue blazes). The trail immediately crosses a wide stream (no bridge), then heads uphill, following the stream. It is a well-used route over scattered rocks. At about the halfway point, a pretty 10-foot

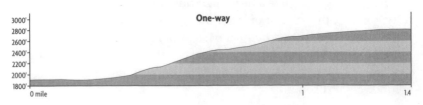

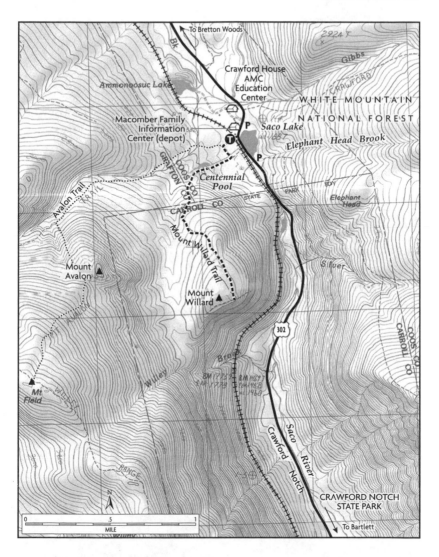

waterfall spills into the Centennial Pool. Your dog will appreciate the short scramble down to the pool, where he can cool off on a hot day.

Shortly after Centennial Pool, the trail bends away from the brook through a spruce corridor, becoming noticeably flatter. It turns to rock slab, then suddenly opens onto a cliff, which is the top. It is a good idea to put your dog on a leash as you approach the summit, particularly if the rock is wet or if the wind is strong. The rock is expansive enough, but the cliff is sheer and could be dangerous to an overly curious dog.

Mount Willey is immediately to the right. Route 302 and the railroad tracks disappear into the notch far below. Mount Chocorua rises like a pyramid in the distance at the end of the notch. Walk to the left for a dramatic view of Mounts Webster, Jackson, Pierce, and Eisenhower (the high rounded peak, farthest to the left), which form the opposite wall of the notch. On a clear day, Mount Washington pokes up beyond Mount Eisenhower.

Centennial Pool on Mount Willard

NORTHERN NEW HAMPSHIRE

26. Mount Cabot–Unknown Pond Loop

Round trip: 11.4 miles entire loop; 9.6 miles Mount Cabot only;
    6.6 miles Unknown Pond only
Hiking time: 1–3 days
High points: 4180 feet (Mount Cabot); 3177 feet (Unknown Pond)
Elevation gain: 3000 feet entire loop; 2700 feet Mount Cabot only;
    1100 feet Unknown Pond only.
Difficulty: 4 paws (strenuous) entire loop or Mount Cabot only;
    2 paws (moderate) Unknown Pond only
Maps: USGS Stark Quad; USGS West Milan Quad; USGS Pliny Range
    Quad
Location: Berlin, NH
Contact: White Mountain National Forest–Androscoggin District,
    603-466-2713, *www.fs.fed.us/r9/white;* for information on fish
    hatchery gate, 603-449-3412

Getting there: From Berlin, take Route 110 West. Turn left on York Pond
Road. Pass through the gate of the fish hatchery and continue another
2 miles past York Pond to the trailheads for both Mount Cabot and
Unknown Pond which are on opposite sides of the road, about 0.1 mile
apart. In summer and fall, the hatchery gate is open from 8:00 AM to 4:00
PM. In winter, it is generally left open. Best parking is at the trailhead for
the Unknown Pond Trail on the right. The trailhead for York Pond Trail,

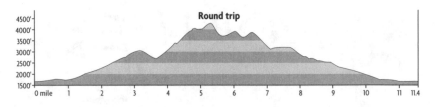

which leads to the Bunnell Notch Trail up Mount Cabot, is slightly farther up the road on the left.

The Mount Cabot–Unknown Pond Loop is actually three possible hikes in one. Besides the entire loop, Mount Cabot and Unknown Pond are both excellent out-and-back hikes in their own right. For peak-baggers, the former is the northernmost 4000-footer in New Hampshire. For water-lovers, the latter is a scenic remote tarn.

When hiked as a loop, there are another two peaks in between—The Bulge and The Horn—north of Mount Cabot along the Kilkenny Ridge. The Bulge (elevation 3920 feet) is a wooded nondescript hump, but The Horn (elevation 3905 feet) is a desirable destination and a viable alternative to Mount Cabot for those who want similar mileage, about 350 feet less vertical, and both a rocky summit and a pond in one hike, neither of which Cabot offers. Do the loop to experience it all.

The loop up Mount Cabot, over The Bulge and The Horn, then down to Unknown Pond can be done as a long day hike, but it might be more appealing as a two- or a three-day backpacking trip. It is described here as a three-day trip. If you decide to try any part of this loop as a day hike, and if you think it will take longer than eight hours to complete the journey, park your car outside the fish hatchery gate, which will add an unwelcome 4 miles to your hike.

Day 1: Trailhead to Cabot Cabin

The York Pond Trail begins as an old grassy road that is now open only to foot traffic. It immediately crosses a stream on a substantial bridge. Keep your dog on the bridge. The banks of the stream are vertical stone walls. If Fido needs a dip, there is a second stream with better access a short way down the trail. This is moose country. There are moose tracks, scat, and other signs of these large beasts everywhere. Keep an eye on your dog. If she picks up even the faintest scent, you should put her on a leash.

At 0.2 mile, at the end of the first small clearing, turn right on the

Bunnell Notch Trail (sporadic yellow blazes), which is also a grassy road. In late August, the road is hemmed with a plethora of wildflowers, including asters, goldenrod, thistles, and daisies. Watch for thorns on the berry bushes and thistles.

At the next small clearing, bear right at the fork. An arrow points the way up massive stone steps, heading toward Mount Cabot, which you can see above the trees. The lower Bunnell Notch Trail is basically flat, crossing several muddy sections, streamlets, and then a more major stream, which is actually the West Branch of the Upper Ammonoosuc River, the source of which is higher on Mount Cabot. Watch for a sign after this crossing directing you left, off the woods road.

The trail continues next to the river crossing and becomes a footpath. It begins climbing, gently at first, then more steadily until it is above the river. Although higher ground, it is still a wet area. The Bunnell Notch Trail has a well-founded reputation for mud. Trail crews recently reworked the larger mud holes with stepping stones and drainage so that they no longer swallow your legs up to the kneecaps, but water-resistant hiking boots are definitely recommended on this hike, even after a week-long drought.

The grades ease again, passing through more muddy areas and crossing a number of streams. The trail seems to undulate upward away from the

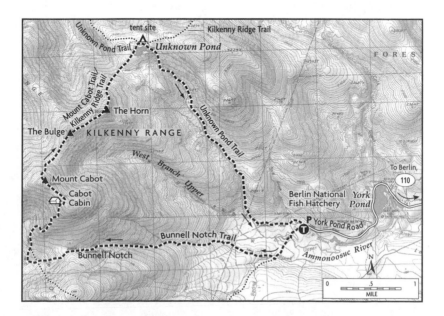

river, then suddenly it is next to the river again. Just when you think the path is drying out, you hit another mud hole. Yet the forest is lush, and the trail, while narrow, is relatively smooth. In general, the Kilkenny area receives much less foot traffic than the mountain ranges to the south, particularly the Presidential Range, which is directly south of Mount Cabot. As a result, the trail is not seriously eroded.

The trail continues to climb in gentle waves, passing through a fern glade. The roaring river eventually fades to a quiet trickle. At 3 miles the trail dips to a junction with the southbound Kilkenny Ridge Trail. Go straight (west) a short way along the plateau. At 3.1 miles turn right onto the northbound Kilkenny Ridge Trail. The path descends slightly as it curls around the mountain. At 3.4 miles the Kilkenny Ridge Trail merges with the Mount Cabot Trail. Stay to the right, keeping the ridge and heading upward. From here to the summit of Cabot, the trail is rockier and older. It is a steady slog up the mountain, which soon becomes tedious if carrying a heavy load, except for the views which appear on the right as the trees begin to shrink. At 3.8 miles a spur to Bunnell Rock offers a view across Bunnell Notch to Terrace, Waumbek, and Starr King Mountains along the southern Kilkenny Ridge.

At 4.4 miles the trail reaches Cabot Cabin, built for the fire-watcher when a tower used to stand atop the mountain. The fire tower was removed in 1965. Today the cabin is maintained by the U.S. Forest Service in cooperation with the local Jefferson Boy Scouts. It is available on a first-come, first-served basis and sleeps eight inside. There is a single tent platform just below it for minor overflow or for those who simply prefer to sleep in a tent. The cabin has an excellent view to the west toward Lancaster. The only downside to the cabin is its water source, a spring located about ten minutes away, toward the summit and then down a steep spur, an effort after the sustained climb to reach the cabin. It is worth bringing enough water to get through the night, then refilling the next day as you continue on.

Day 2: Cabot Cabin to Unknown Pond

The next morning, pick up the trail around the back of the cabin. It is a moderate climb to the wooded summit of Mount Cabot at 4.8 miles, where the footings of the old fire tower remain. There are two lookouts to the left, with views to the west over low fir trees. From the summit the trail bends right and drops off, becoming much steeper, narrower, and softer. Roots crisscross the path, which soon begins to climb up

Cabot Cabin

The Bulge. The summit of The Bulge is discernible only because the trail crests there. Some trees are dead among the firs, and the forest is more open.

The trail bends to the right over The Bulge, continuing along the ridge. At 5.6 miles another spur departs right to the top of The Horn. The climb is only 0.3 mile and 255 vertical feet to the summit, but it is a scramble. At the first rocky area, head through the rocks with your dog. (The seemingly easier way to the left has a rock wall around the corner that is too high for a dog.) The last short scramble requires climbing over a few large rocks. The Horn is only for the most agile canines. It is worth the effort. The view is the best of the hike! Look back over The Bulge to Mount Cabot and other nearby mountains layered into the mist.

Retrace your steps, reaching the Kilkenny Ridge Trail again at 6.5 miles, then turn right. The trail drops below the ridge for a time, hugging the mountain as it traverses, then it descends toward the pond. It is rough at first, but becomes smoother about the point where the birch trees make their way back into the forest mix. The trail continues through a sag, crossing a mud hole on split logs, then rising to a height of land where it crosses another mud hole on another log walkway.

At 8.1 miles, Unknown Pond appears on your right just before reaching the junction with the Unknown Pond Trail. As the name implies, Unknown Pond is a quiet, secluded tarn. It is dotted with lily pads and surrounded by a rugged, wooded shoreline, although a few footpaths allow access to the water here and there. The pointed peak of The Horn crowns its southwestern shore. It is an easy place to spend an afternoon and an evening. Your dog will undoubtedly enjoy a swim in its calm waters. There are several primitive campsites along the side of the pond near the intersection of the Kilkenny Ridge Trail and the Unknown Pond Trail, with rarely any competition for them. There are also designated campsites and an outhouse farther along the Unknown Pond Trail. Please follow the principles of Leave-No-Trace when using any campsites near Unknown Pond.

Day 3: Unknown Pond to the Trailhead

Amid the half-dozen campsites the trail forks, heading left (uphill) to continue northeast along the Kilkenny Ridge Trail or right (level) toward York Pond. Take the right fork, bending south and east around the end of the pond.

At first the trail descends through a fern and birch glade, but soon a garden of wildflowers takes over. The best time to see the riot of blooms is in mid- to late August. The trail crosses several streamlets, entering a more classic northern forest. The forest is airy with many maples in the mix, making this hike an excellent choice during fall foliage.

The trail drops down a short steep slope, helped by a few stone steps, then follows a substantial brook on the right, a tributary of the West Branch of the Upper Ammonoosuc River. After crossing the brook, the trail continues down the opposite bank, then crosses back to the original side. The descent is gentle and smooth. For this reason, the hike out and back to Unknown Pond gets a 2-paw rating (moderate), despite its 3-paw distance (6.6 miles round trip).

As you continue down, the brook gains momentum on your right and soon builds to a constant roar. The trail passes through several mud holes (although nothing as extensive as on the Bunnell Notch Trail) and over a few more log bridges. It finally meanders out of the woods at 11.4 miles.

27. North Percy

Round trip: 4.4 miles
Hiking time: 3.5 hours
High point: 3418 feet
Elevation gain: 2140 feet
Difficulty: 3 paws (ambitious)
Map: USGS Percy Peaks Quad
Location: Nash Stream Forest; northeast of Groveton, NH
Contact: New Hampshire Division of Parks and Recreation,
603-271-3254, *www.nhstateparks.org;* Cohos Trail Association,
603-363-8902, *www.cohostrail.org*

Getting there: From Groveton, travel east on Route 110. Turn left on Emerson Road. Turn right on Northside Road, then left on Nash Stream Road. The trailhead is on your right just after Slide Brook (noted by sign). Best parking is just south of Slide Brook at the small designated parking area.

The view of the Percy Peaks from Route 110 is striking. They rise like twin cones across the Upper Ammonoosuc River, but they are not identical. North Percy is the more open peak, gleaming white in the sunlight. South Percy is covered with trees. Only the route up North Percy is described here, as it is by far the more scenic summit of the two.

The hike up North Percy is fairly short on mileage, but big on vertical. In addition, the trail is washed out in sections and traverses a lot of low-angle slab. It is fine for dogs and humans that are seasoned hikers, but this is probably not your best choice if you and your dog are just breaking in your hiking legs. That said, it has a spectacular open summit, and the climb, though steep and challenging in places, is interesting for its variety. It is best to avoid this hike when conditions are wet or icy, as the extensive rocky areas will be treacherous.

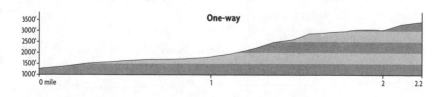

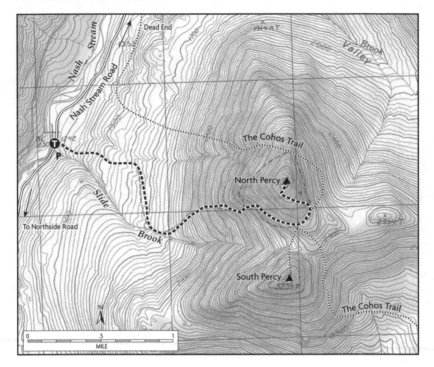

The trail enters the woods across a couple of wooden planks, heading up the left bank of Slide Brook. Although the white blazes are intermittent at best, the trail is smooth and obvious as it climbs moderately through the northern forest. There is a lot of dog-friendly water on the lower part of this hike. The trail draws away from the stream as it climbs but soon swings back toward it, crossing a tributary on an old log bridge at 0.3 mile. It resumes its climb, paralleling the brook again atop a shallow ravine.

At about 1 mile, the trail bends left around an immense boulder capped with several scruffy spruce trees. Beyond the boulder the trail is much rougher, like a dry streambed. It climbs steeply up an embankment, then continues on an aggressive ascent over rocks and roots, leaving Slide Brook behind.

About ten minutes later, the trail reaches its first length of slab. Although it is still under the canopy, the canopy is considerably lower. The official route is up the right side of the slab over a gnarl of roots. A few moments later, a rope, fixed to the top of another length of slab, dangles

Opposite: Flag on a hiking pole, "planted" on the summit of North Percy

to help humans, although both people and dogs will find it easier to climb up the right side of the rock on a ribbon of dirt. A view begins to emerge behind you to the west from the top of the rock.

The trail bends to the right and the grade eases, as it angles ever upward, now surrounded by softwoods. At the next section of low-angle slab, the best route is again on the right, up a vague path of dirt and roots. Humans might prefer the short friction climb, but dogs will likely follow the tree line.

The ascent continues through the trees. After crossing a section of narrow side-hill slab, the route becomes more trail-like again through an open glade of birch and fir trees. At about 1.4 miles, the trail squeezes between two large rocks (one rock cracked in two long ago), then up a long rock shelf. It bends left at the end of the shelf, slowly curving in a more easterly direction and on the best footing since the bottom of the hike.

At about 1.7 miles the first yellow Cohos Trail blazes appear in the notch between the two Percy peaks. A few minutes later, the trail reaches a fork with the Percy Loop Trail. Bear left for North Percy.

From the fork, the trail is relatively easy going except for a couple of high rock "steps," which pose little problem for a retriever-size dog. It climbs a short, steep washout, then breaks from the trees, covering the final few vertical feet on open slab. The rock is dotted with low evergreens and blueberry bushes. Follow the vague red blazes and small cairns for the best route to the top.

The summit looks like a sharp peak from Route 110, but it is actually broad and flat, about a half acre in size. There is a 360-degree view, but it helps to walk to different sides of the summit to see it due to the low, scattered trees. A small American flag tied to a trekking pole is cemented in place on the eastern side of the summit. The view is among the best north of the Presidential Range. New Hampshire's highest peaks are visible to the south like rows of blue spires as far as the eye can see. Northern Vermont lies to the west. Canada is on the northern horizon, and the wilderness to the east extends into Maine.

PART 3

Vermont

Then, as now, we did not believe that a dog's place was in the city.

—*Kurt Unkelbach*
Source: *Those Lovable Retrievers*
(McGraw-Hill, 1973)

SOUTHERN VERMONT

28. Mount Equinox

Round trip: 5.8 miles
Hiking time: 4.5 hours
High point: 3852 feet
Elevation gain: 2882 feet
Difficulty: 3 paws (ambitious)
Map: USGS Manchester Quad
Location: Manchester, VT
Contact: Green Mountain Club, 802-244-7037, *www.greenmountainclub
.org;* Green Mountain National Forest–Manchester District, 802-362-
2307, *www.fs.fed.us/r9/gmfl/*

Getting there: Take Route 7A south from Manchester Center. Turn right
on Seminary Avenue. Best parking is either in the upper lot of Burr and
Burton Seminary (when school is not in session), or continue up the hill,
turn right on West Union Street, and park near the gate.

Manchester, Vermont, is wedged into a narrow valley formed by the Green
Mountains to the east and the Taconic Mountains to the west. Mount
Equinox, which towers over the village, is the highest peak in the Taconic

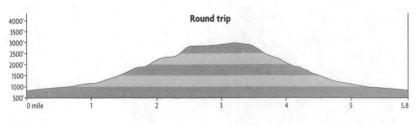

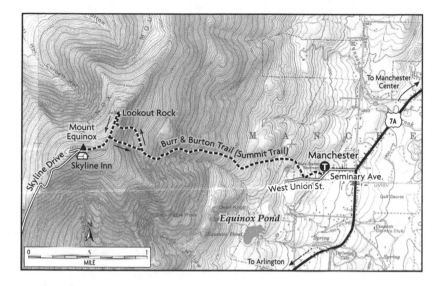

Range. It is the dominant peak on the west side of Manchester and the highest peak in Vermont that is not part of the Green Mountains.

The hike up Mount Equinox is worthwhile for its excellent views, both from Lookout Rock which lies northeast of the true summit along the summit ridge, and from the summit itself. The hike described here is a "lollipop hike," with a loop at the top encompassing the summit and Lookout Rock.

From the Manchester side, the most direct and canine-compatible route is via the Burr & Burton Trail, also known as the "Summit Trail." The blue-blazed trail is accessible at the top of the uppermost sports field behind Burr and Burton Seminary. It is part of a web of trails, all color-coded, that originate at the Mount Equinox Hotel. There is nothing particularly difficult about this well-maintained trail, except that it climbs quite steadily for an extended period of time, so expect a good cardiac workout. And there is little water, except for one spring, accessible by a spur trail about halfway up the mountain. Be sure to carry enough for both you and your dog.

The Burr & Burton Trail begins as a multi-use woods road, climbing gently through a hardwood forest. Within minutes it reaches a gate at the top of a dirt road (West Union Street). Walk around the gate and continue straight up the road, following the red and blue blazes. A few minutes later, the Red Trail exits to the left. Continue straight on the Blue Trail, soon passing a green cabin and crossing the Trillium Trail.

After the next intersection, with the Maidenhair Trail, the climb really

Large hollow tree beside trail on Mount Equinox

begins. Although the trail is still road-like, it becomes somewhat rockier, climbing steadily and winding up the mountain at long angles. As you begin to gain altitude, the path levels off briefly and narrows through a corridor of birch saplings, then comes to a fork at 1.6 miles. At this point, the Upper Spring Trail (purple) continues straight; the Summit Trail bends sharply uphill. Continue climbing on the Summit Trail, now a rocky footpath that generally hugs the mountain in a westerly direction. At about 2 miles the trail takes a noticeable turn to the right and the grade finally eases as it enters softwoods. Soon it takes another sharp bend to the right, crossing a short mud flat and reaching a plateau.

At a four-way intersection, turn right, traversing in a northeasterly direction toward Lookout Rock. (You will descend via the trail straight ahead from the summit back to this point.) There are several faded yellow and red blazes on the trees along the way. At 2.7 miles the trail reaches the summit ridge where signs point out the Red Trail and the Yellow Trail, heading the same way along two parallel woods roads. Take the road on the right (yellow blazes). At 3.1 miles the trail ends at a bench at Lookout Rock (elevation 3673 feet), with an expansive view to the east and the village of Manchester directly below.

From Lookout Rock, follow the other path in the opposite direction, ignoring the intersection with the Beartown Gap Trail which descends to the right, toward Dorset. Continue past the next intersection, with the trail on which you came up.

At 3.5 miles the trail reaches a small clearing with a large tombstone on the left. The stone is in memory of "Mr. Barbo," a Norwegian elkhound–Siberian husky mix that was shot by a hunter in 1955. Mr. Barbo was owned by Joseph Davidson, the former president and CEO of Union Carbide, who at one point owned the entire mountain and who built the toll-road back in the late 1940s.

From the tombstone, the trail bears slightly right (west) past a small radio tower, over a stretch of slab and up a gentle rise. At 3.6 miles the trail passes a larger radio tower and ends at the Skyline Inn, an unused motel at the summit of the mountain. When the summit is in the clouds, the inn appears ghostly—in perfect condition, but abandoned. The toll road ends on the other side of the inn.

To complete the summit loop, retrace your steps to the larger radio tower, then follow the trail behind the tower, which descends directly to the Blue Trail. It meets the Blue Trail at the four-way intersection mentioned earlier. Retrace your steps from here back to your car.

29. Haystack Mountain

Round trip: 4.8 miles
Hiking time: 3 hours
High point: 3420 feet
Elevation gain: 1020 feet
Difficulty: 2 paws (moderate)
Map: USGS Mount Snow Quad
Location: Wilmington, VT
Contact: Green Mountain National Forest–Manchester District,
802-362-2307, *www.fs.fed.us/r9/gmfl/*

Getting there: From Route 9 west of Wilmington, turn onto Chimney Hill Road, which makes a sharp 90-degree turn in the midst of a housing development. Turn right on Binney Brook Road and follow it uphill. Turn left on Upper Dam Road. The trailhead and parking are on the right just after the turn.

There are at least three Haystack Mountains in Vermont with trails on them: one to the far north near Jay Peak, one near Lake Willoughby (also north), and the other to the far south by Mount Snow. The trail described here is the southernmost one.

From a skier's point of view, Haystack Mountain, a satellite ski area to giant Mount Snow, is of little consequence. But from a hiker's point of view, Haystack offers more dog-friendly hiking, particularly since Mount Snow's trail system is a mecca for mountain bikers. The hike up the Haystack Mountain Trail is primarily wooded and relatively gradual the entire way, making it a perfect hike for pups and older dogs.

The trail begins on a gravel road. Walk around the gate partway up the initial incline, which serves to keep motor traffic out. At 0.4 mile, turn left over a streamlet off the woods road and onto a wide footpath. The trail descends gently through a muddy sag, then begins to climb. After

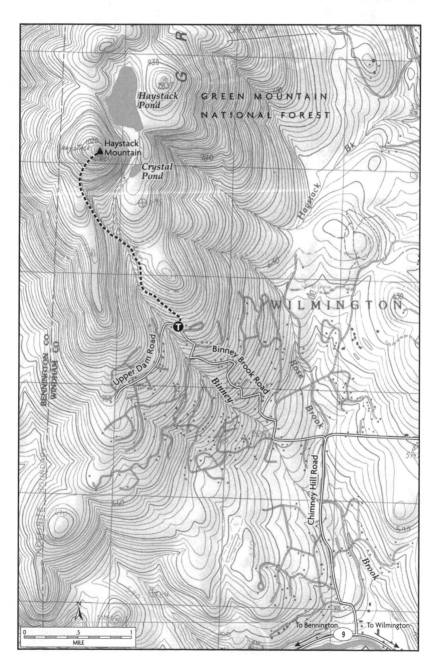

Bella and Patriot get a treat on top of Haystack Mountain.

a moderate ascent through a hardwood forest, the trail levels off in a northerly direction. At about 1 mile the trail resumes a gentle ascent, bending to the right and following blue markers shaped like diamonds. At about 1.6 miles it flattens again on another plateau. There is a break in the canopy, and a blackberry "hedge" frames the trail. Before long, the trail crosses another muddy area, then ascends a moderate pitch and becomes noticeably rockier, often with water trickling underfoot.

At 2 miles a small rock cairn in the middle of the trail marks a junction. A yellow arrow points the way to the summit, a right turn up the steeper slope. The trail soon swings to the right and moderates again, winding up the hill. At 2.4 miles the foliage turns to fir and meets a large rock. Walk over it to find the top!

The view is an eastern panorama. Haystack Pond lies about 500 feet below. Mount Monadnock in New Hampshire is straight ahead. The summit of Mount Snow and its ski trails are to the far left, with Killington and the Coolidge Range visible beyond on a clear day. Wachusett and Greylock lie to the south.

30. Mount Olga

Round trip: 1.7 miles
Hiking time: 2 hours
High point: 2145 feet
Elevation gain: 520 feet
Difficulty: 1 paw (easy)
Fees and permits: Day use fee, $2.50 adults, $2 children ages 4–13
Pet policy: You must show proof of rabies vaccination at the ranger cabin; dogs must be attended and on a leash no longer than ten feet at all times; dogs must be quiet
Maps: USGS Wilmington Quad; USGS Jacksonville Quad
Location: Molly Stark State Park; Wilmington, VT
Contact: Vermont Department of Forests, Parks & Recreation, 802-464-5460 (park phone, mid-May to mid-October), *www.vtstateparks.com*

Getting there: From Wilmington, VT, head east on Route 9 for about 4 miles. The entrance to the state park is on the south side of the road. Best parking is at the ranger cabin and picnic area.

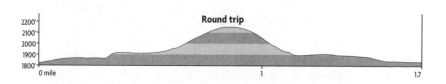

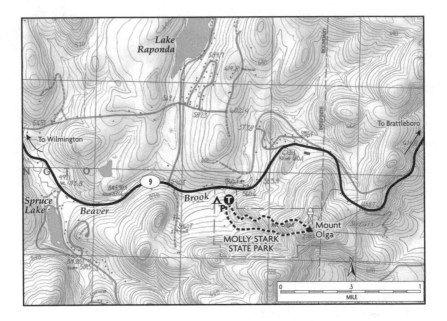

Mount Olga is located in Molly Stark State Park. The woman for whom the mountain is named is unknown, but the woman for whom the state park is named—Molly Stark—is legendary. Molly Stark was born Elizabeth Page in 1737. She was nicknamed "Molly" by her husband, John Stark, who became a brigadier general in the New Hampshire Militia (which included Vermont during colonial times). In 1777, during the Battle of Bennington, Stark sent a message to his wife, "Send every man from the farm that will come, and let the haying go to hell." Molly not only complied, but also recruited several hundred other men to aid her husband. Then she converted the Stark barn into a hospital to care for the wounded from both the American and the British sides.

The hike up Mount Olga is not nearly as tenacious as Molly Stark. In fact, it is an easy loop, but with a big reward—a fire tower with a 360-degree view of southern Vermont and northern Massachusetts. Because it is so accessible, this hike can be crowded on weekends, so plan a midweek outing with a dog.

The trail leaves the picnic area from the right side of the ranger cabin on the Mount Olga Trail (blue blazes). The start of the trail is mulched with wood chips and immediately dips over a bridge before climbing through an open mixed forest. At 0.1 mile it crosses an old stone wall, then turns left, heading along the wall for about thirty yards. Then the trail turns right, continuing up the hillside. Roots crisscross the well-marked path, but the footing is still easy.

The trail enters a grove of softwoods, dips, then levels off as it winds through the forest. At about 0.5 mile it comes to a bench with another stone wall behind it. The path crosses the wall, then continues to climb gently, soon passing a tree that was struck by lightning in 2003. Today, the tree looks oddly delaminated, with strips of trunk arcing over the trail.

The trail climbs more steadily through a switchback to the left, before resuming its casual climb. At 0.7 mile you come to a T; bear left, climbing over a stretch of slab and passing three rundown cabins, from the days when Mount Olga was known as the Hogback Ski Area. At 0.8 mile, just past the cabins, the fire tower and a separate, lower communications tower glint against the sky.

When you climb the tower, the view transports you away from the summit clutter. The sweeping view is mesmerizing, with hills that roll on forever in every direction. The original tower was constructed in 1930. The current one was moved to Mount Olga from nearby Bald Mountain in 1949, and remained in active service until the 1970s. It is registered as a National Historic Lookout. Please leave your dog at the bottom of the tower on a leash.

To continue the loop, retrace your steps back to the junction at 0.9 mile. Go straight across the top of the T. The route downhill is similar to the uphill one in terms of scenery and grade. At 1.6 miles go straight at the junction, following a stone wall. When the trail meets the road that circles the camping area, turn right and follow the road a short way back to the parking lot.

Fire tower on Mount Olga

31. Stratton Mountain–Stratton Pond Loop

Total distance: 10.6 miles (with a car drop); 11.5 miles (without a
car drop)

Hiking time: 7 hours or overnight

High point: 3936 feet

Elevation gain: 1910 feet

Difficulty: 3 paws (ambitious)

Fees and permits: $5 per night per person to camp at Stratton Pond;
camping is not permitted on Stratton Mountain or within 0.5
mile of Stratton Pond, except at designated sites

Map: USGS Stratton Mountain Quad

Location: Stratton, VT

Contact: Green Mountain Club, 802-244-7037, *www.greenmountainclub*
.org; Green Mountain National Forest–Manchester District, 802-362-
2307, *www.fs.fed.us/r9/gmfl/*

Getting there, AT/LT trailhead (recommended start): From the village
of Stratton (not the resort), head west toward Arlington on the Arlington–West Wardsboro Road, also called the Kelley Stand Road. (This road
is closed during the winter.) The trailhead for the Appalachian Trail/Long
Trail (AT/LT) is on the right about 3 miles from Stratton, just beyond the
trailhead for Grout Pond.

To **Stratton Pond Trail trailhead (end of hike):** Continue past the
AT/LT trailhead for another mile. The trailhead for the Stratton Pond
Trail is on the right.

Stratton Mountain has three claims to fame. It is the tallest peak in
southern Vermont, and the ideas for both the Long Trail (LT) and the
Appalachian Trail (AT) originated here. In 1909 James Taylor envisioned
a "long trail" that would link the main peaks of the Green Mountains
from the Massachusetts border to the Canadian border. Twelve years later,

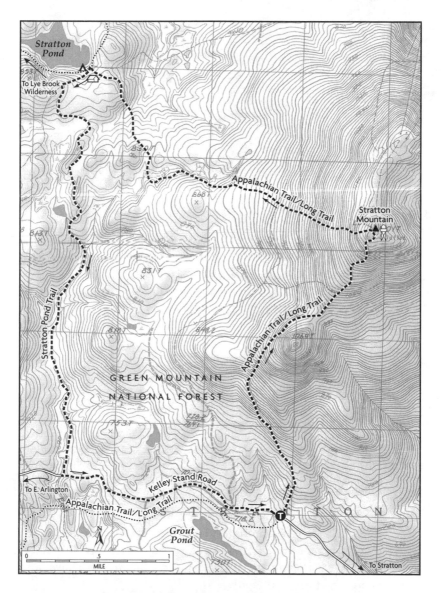

Benton MacKaye expanded the idea to encompass the entire Appalachian Mountain chain from Georgia to Maine.

The route to the summit is described here, continuing down to scenic Stratton Pond via the AT/LT (white blazes) then back to the Kelley Stand Road via the Stratton Pond Trail. It is a long day mileage-wise, but the footing is excellent and the climb is not steep. This route is not a perfect

Duckboards, also called puncheon or bog bridges, on the Stratton Pond Trail

loop, as the Stratton Pond Trail ends 0.9 mile from the AT/LT trailhead. A car drop is a helpful option. After hiking over 10 miles, it is nice to ride rather than walk the extra mile along the Kelley Stand Road to close the circle.

Heading north on the AT/LT from the parking area, the trail quickly comes to a fork. Bear right, following the white blazes, traversing a muddy area. At about 0.4 mile the trail crosses a streamlet and starts to climb gently along a woods road. The trail crosses several duckboards (also called "bog bridges" or "puncheons") as it meanders through the woods, traversing slightly downhill toward the mountain. Watch the blazes carefully in this area, as many old logging roads cross the trail.

At about 1.2 miles, the trail bends to the right (east) and climbs gently again over a knoll as it continues to approach the mountain. It crosses another logging road and several streamlets (sometimes dry) as it dips and bends, sometimes climbing, sometimes flat.

At about 1.9 miles the climb becomes steeper over chunks of rock, then flattens again as it travels along a hillside, back on its northern track. By 2.9 miles it reaches an upland plateau where the trees are lower and thinner and soon turn coniferous.

The miles seem to melt away on the ascent to the summit, as nothing about the trail is remotely vertical or strenuous. By 3.6 miles the trail gets rockier, then passes a white cabin, reserved for a caretaker from the Green Mountain Club. The fire tower is directly ahead across an elongated grassy clearing at 3.8 miles.

The Stratton fire tower was built in 1914. The original lookout cabin was replaced in 1934 with the current one. It is a designated National Historic Landmark. As always, dogs should not go up the fire tower. From the small metal cabin fifty-five feet above the ground, you can see the top of the ski area's gondola, 0.8 mile away on Stratton's north peak. The view from the tower extends into five states. Key landmarks include Mount Snow to the south, Mount Monadnock in New Hampshire to the southeast, Mount Ascutney to the northeast, and Mount Equinox to the west. Your next stop, Stratton Pond, is visible to the northwest.

Turn left past the fire tower to begin the descent to Stratton Pond. At about 4.1 miles the trail arcs to the left down wooden steps, winding off the peak at a moderate grade and reentering the hardwoods. By 5 miles it dips over a stream (unreliable) and crosses a swampy area on duckboards. Dogs will love to wallow in the chest-deep pool of water on the right. At about 5.8 miles, the trail bends to the west, then crosses a logging road. It traverses a long, muddy area, eventually crossing a stream on a bridge. From there it climbs gently to a fork with an older trail. Bear right at the fork, heading uphill.

After more mud and duckboards, the trail comes to a T at about 6.8 miles, meeting the Stratton Pond Trail. Turn right toward Stratton Pond, continuing on the AT/LT north. It is a short way to a grassy clearing at the water's edge, where your dog will likely bound in for a swim.

Stratton Pond seems more like a small lake than a pond. It is the largest body of water on the Long Trail. It also receives the heaviest use, but midweek, especially after Labor Day, the chances are good that no one will be there. Camping is only allowed at the designated shelter and tent sites. The Green Mountain Club has a caretaker at the pond during the summer, who collects the $5 overnight fee.

To reach the shelter, backtrack the short distance to the junction of the AT/LT and the Stratton Pond Trail. Continue straight (south) on the Stratton Pond Trail (blue blazes). At the top of the next rise, the trail turns right. The short spur to the Stratton Pond Shelter is straight ahead.

To complete the loop, continue south on the Stratton Pond Trail. At 7.9 miles the trail crosses the first of many duckboards as it heads gently downward. By about 9 miles it crosses a woods road, then continues its long traverse over more duckboards, finally reaching the trailhead at 10.6 miles on the Kelley Stand Road.

WEST-CENTRAL VERMONT

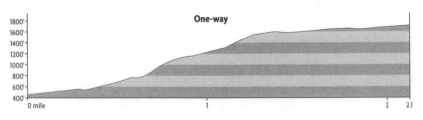

32. Abbey Pond

Round trip: 4.2 miles
Hiking time: 2.5 hours
High point: 1700 feet
Elevation gain: 1200 feet
Difficulty: 2 paws (moderate)
Map: USGS South Mountain Quad
Location: East Middlebury, VT
Contact: Green Mountain National Forest–Middlebury District, 802-388-4362; *www.fs.fed.us/r9/gmfl/*

Getting there: From East Middlebury, head north on Route 116 toward Bristol. Go about 4.2 miles, then turn right at the brown sign for the "Abbey Pond Trail." The road forks immediately. Bear right, then continue straight ahead on this dirt road for about 0.4 mile, which leads into the parking area. The trailhead is at the back of the parking lot.

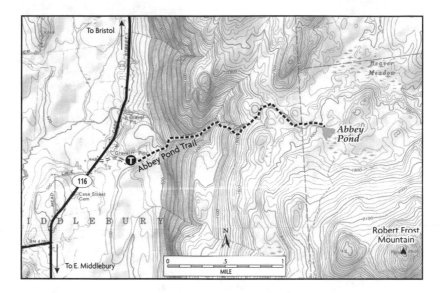

The Abbey Pond Trail (blue blazes) enters the woods on a gravel path. At first it climbs gently, with dense hardwood forest to either side but open sky above. At about 0.1 mile a boulder on the left appears sliced into sections. More large boulders dot the woods, then the trail crosses an old stone wall. The path becomes somewhat steeper, and the gravel gives way to loose rocks. The trail bends to the left, then at 0.2 mile crosses a scenic brook on a solid footbridge. Cascades tumble down a small gorge on the right, then flow over smooth ledges to the left. If the water levels are low, there are a couple of shallow pools here that your dog will enjoy.

The moderate climb continues on a woods road, basically paralleling the brook. It is a lovely setting. The trail passes a number of cascades. The surrounding woods are dotted with interesting boulders and rocky outcroppings. Large trees cling impossibly to the tops of rocks. At 0.6 mile, the trail re-crosses the brook, this time sans bridge. There is a narrow gap between two boulders on the opposite shores—the driest step for humans. Dogs will surely take advantage of the crossing to play in the water.

The trail continues along the hillside, then arcs right, away from the brook before resuming its steady climb. A few minutes later it bends back to the left and the grade eases. The woods seem less dense than near the trailhead. After a long traverse, the trail eventually returns to the brook. At about 1.4 miles it crosses the brook again by a large, shallow pool.

Bravo retrieves a chunk of wood near the shore of Abbey Pond.

From here, the trail narrows to a traditional footpath, first arcing to the left, then snaking through the woods over flat terrain.

After a quarter-mile traverse south, the trail crosses a muddy section and arrives at Abbey Pond at 2.1 miles. There is no path around the pond, but a large, rocky outcropping on the right lends itself for picnicking. The pond's shoreline is dotted with beaver dams, and Robert Frost Mountain graces the far end of its expanse to the southeast. Abbey Pond is particularly pleasant during fall foliage season, when the entire shoreline turns red and orange.

Note: If herons are nesting on Abbey Pond, the trail may be closed. If you are planning this hike during the spring or early summer, it is worth calling ahead to see if the trail is open. Also, if beavers are swimming in the pond, please prevent your dog from chasing them.

33. Killington Peak

Round trip: 7.2 miles
Hiking time: 5 hours
High point: 4241 feet
Elevation gain: 2480 feet
Difficulty: 4 paws (strenuous)
Fees and permits: $5 overnight fee to sleep at Cooper Lodge
Map: USGS Killington Peak Quad
Location: Mendon, VT
Contact: Green Mountain Club (GMC), 802-244-7037,
www.greenmountainclub.org

Getting there: From Route 4, turn onto Wheelerville Road (dirt) about 5 miles east of Rutland. Continue 4 miles, passing the Rutland Watershed Area on your left. When the road makes a 90-degree turn to the right, look for the pullout on the left. (Note: You must approach the trailhead from Route 4. A section of the Wheelerville Road washed out during spring 2004, with no plans for its repair.)

Killington Peak is the second highest mountain in Vermont. It is the highest of the six peaks that make up Killington Resort. Best known for skiing in the winter, the resort encourages hiking up its ski-trails and publishes a trail map for hikers, with ten self-guided interpretive hikes across five of the six peaks. However, you are more likely to have a true wilderness experience with your dog on the opposite side of the mountain via the Bucklin Trail (blue blazes), a traditional hiking trail.

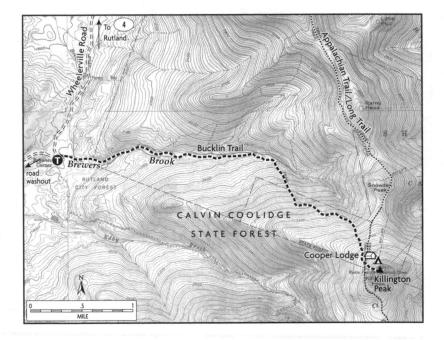

From the parking area, the trail begins on a woods road shared with the Catamount Trail, which mainly serves snowmobilers and cross-country skiers during in the winter. The Catamount Trail is also marked in blue, but with small plastic diamonds. Ignore them. Stick to the blue painted blazes.

The woods road immediately crosses Brewers Brook over a bridge, then follows the brook, gradually rising away from it. It narrows to a footpath, lined with a kaleidoscope of wildflowers in early summer. At 0.8 mile it re-crosses the brook, continuing up the other side and distancing itself from the water. The next streamlet is your dog's last chance to cool off before the real climb.

At 1.8 miles the Bucklin Trail intersects with an unnamed evacuation route, which the Killington ski patrol uses in winter for injured back-country skiers. The evacuation route is blocked by a low dirt berm. Bear right up the hill. From here the trail rises steeply through a hardwood forest above a carpet of ferns. When you start to see ridge line through the tree tops, watch for an unusual twisted tree next to the trail. It is about three feet in diameter and has a huge hollow—big enough to stand in—on its uphill side.

The trail finally flattens out briefly as you enter a subalpine area where the trees turn coniferous. At 3.4 miles the Bucklin Trail reaches the Appalachian Trail/Long Trail (AT/LT, white blazes). Continue up, not left, on the AT/LT. From here on, the footing is more rooted, while the ascent is more moderate.

At the next fork, a sign points right to a water source, but turn left to reach Cooper Lodge, a cabin maintained by the Green Mountain Club (GMC). Constructed of stone and wood, the lodge is relatively spacious with sleeping platforms that hold up to sixteen people and a full-sized picnic table. The entire northwestern side of the cabin has windows, redefining the cliché, "a room with a view."

Cooper Lodge was built in 1939 by the Vermont Forest Service. It is located on state land donated by Mortimer R. Proctor, a former president of the GMC and a governor of Vermont, in honor of Charles P. Cooper, another former president of the club. The GMC is considering removal of this shelter, which is the object of frequent vandalism and abuse due to its easy access from the ski area, so backpackers should check with the GMC first before assuming they can sleep there. A GMC Ridgerunner may collect $5 per person for overnight use of the lodge.

If the cabin is full, bear right up the log steps, to find a number of tent platforms in the woods just above the cabin. From there the trail climbs a short but steep and rocky 0.2 mile to Killington Peak. The rocks feel like steps prepared for giants rather than humans, but dogs seem to have no trouble on them.

While the summit is not expansive, it is bare and well worth the climb, particularly for the view north, which extends into the other high peaks of the Green Mountains

Hollow tree beside the Bucklin Trail up Killington Peak

as far as Mount Mansfield. Blue Mountain lies to the left of Pico Peak, framing the Chittenden Reservoir with the spine of the Green Mountains. To the west lies tree-covered Little Killington in the foreground, with Bald Mountain and the Rutland valley farther away. On a clear day, look through the gap at the far side of Rutland to the Adirondacks. To catch Mount Ascutney to the southeast, you have to look through the jumble of communication equipment on an old fire tower. The fire tower is not open to the public. The rocky trail beyond the summit leads to the Killington gondola only 200 yards away. Many people ride up the gondola, then make the short hike from there to the summit. Unless your dog is very social, it is best to hike this mountain midweek, when tourist traffic up the gondola is less.

34. Okemo (Ludlow) Mountain

Round trip: 5.8 miles
Hiking time: 3–4 hours
High point: 3343 feet
Elevation gain: 1943 feet
Difficulty: 3 paws (ambitious)
Pet policy: Keep pets under control
Map: USGS Mount Holly Quad
Location: Mount Holly, VT
Contact: Okemo State Forest, 802-885-8855; Vermont Department of
   Forests, Parks and Recreation, 802-886-2215, *www.vtstateparks.com*

Getting there: From the main entrance to the Okemo Mountain Resort in Ludlow, take Route 103 north for 4 miles. Turn left on Station Road. After crossing the railroad tracks, look for the parking lot and the trailhead on the left.

The Healdville Trail (blue blazes) is the main hiking trail to the top of Okemo Mountain, which is slightly higher than the ski area. Built by the Vermont Youth Conservation Corps, the Healdville Trail is now managed

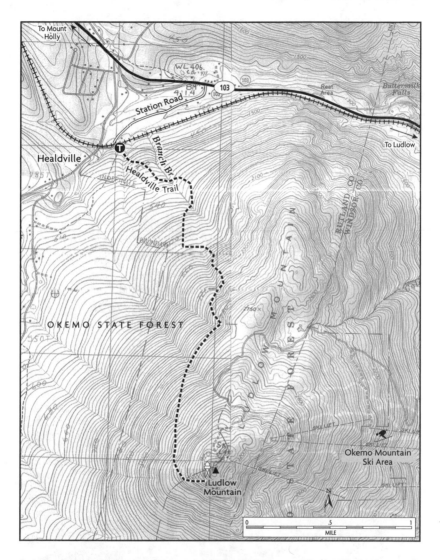

by the State of Vermont as part of the 7500-acre Okemo State Forest. It is well maintained with real footbridges, rather than the usual two logs anchored in place. It starts over the first of these bridges before heading into a hardwood forest. The footing is easy, and the trail is wide. It quickly crosses a second stream, then heads uphill in earnest along the left the side of Branch Brook. The brook tumbles over a number of small waterfalls forming a series of tiny pools, each a perfect resting spot where your dog can cool off on a hot day.

The trail climbs steadily for about 1.5 miles before finally reaching a flat section and a chance for a normal heart rate. At this point, it bears right and traverses the mountain to the south for another 0.4 mile to a sign for the Healdville Trail. A side trail seems to turn left, uphill, at the sign; go straight, continuing on the traverse.

The trail dips down over a clear, rocky stream with a nice pool just

Stone chimney and foundation from the old fire-watcher's cabin on Okemo Mountain

below the crossing area. This is another good place for a break for both you and your dog if you need it. From there, the trail heads up again. Just below the summit, you will pass a stone chimney and the stone outline of the old watchman's cabin before coming to the intersection with the trail that leads to the Mountain Road parking lot. Turn right to reach the fire tower.

The summit of Okemo is below tree line, but the tall fire tower gives a spectacular 360-degree view, including Mount Washington and the White Mountains to the northeast, Mount Ascutney closer and south of the Whites, and Mount Monadnock in the distance beyond the chairlift terminal. From the other side of the tower (opposite the ski area), you can see a significant part of the main ridge of Green Mountains to the west.

Do not take your dog up the steps of the fire tower. Keep him tied on a leash while you climb the tower, avoiding the area directly around its base; be alert for small glass shards on the rocks that could cut his paws.

35. Pico Peak

Round trip: 5.8 miles
Hiking time: 3.5 hours
High point: 3957 feet
Elevation gain: 1807 feet
Difficulty: 4 paws (strenuous)
Fees and permits: $5 overnight fee to sleep in Pico Shelter
Map: USGS Pico Peak Quad
Location: Killington, VT
Contact: Green Mountain Club (GMC), 802-244-7037,
    www.greenmountainclub.org; Green Mountain National Forest–
    Rochester District, 802-767-4261, *www.fs.fed.us/r9/gmfl/*

Getting there: Take Route 4 to the top of Sherburne Pass, west of the entrance to the Pico Ski Area. The trailhead begins at the end of the parking lot on the south side of the road, across the street from the Inn at Long Trail.

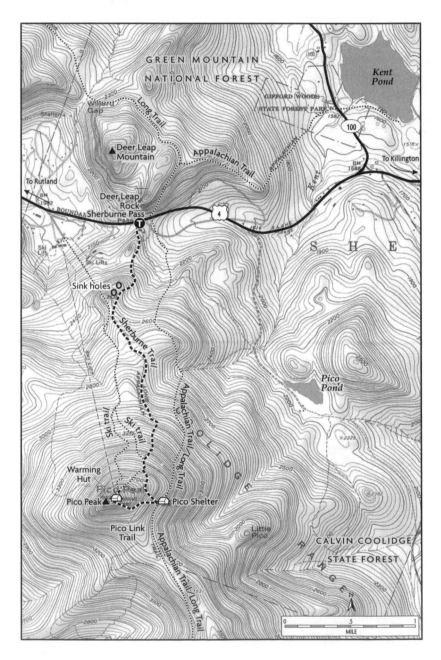

The Sherburne Pass Trail (blue blazes) dates back to 1913, when it was built as the original Long Trail (LT) through this area. Several years ago, the LT was moved slightly west to accommodate a potential ski area expansion, which has not happened yet. Do not be alarmed if the trailhead parking lot seems full of cars, even midweek. Most hikers head to Deer Leap on the opposite side of Route 4. The hike up Pico can also be busy, particularly on weekends, but midweek is typically less populated and perfect for a dog-hike now that the LT has been relocated.

From the sign-in box, the well-worn trail heads up moderately through a hardwood forest, with a lush understory of ferns, low leafy shrubs, wood sorrel, and grasses. The footing is a New England mix of rocks, roots, and rock slab. Ignore the first unmarked but obvious spur to the right; it merely leads to a ski area work road with no view.

At 1 mile the trail enters a maple grove. At 1.3 miles it passes two sinkholes on the right. It is best to put your dog on a leash as you pass the sinkholes. The first is smaller, about seven feet deep. The second is twice the size, with two short unofficial footpaths and a small streamlet leading into it. Both you and your dog should avoid exploring the sinkholes. The soil can be unstable around them, and both are part of a small cave that is unsafe for novice spelunking.

After the sinkholes the trail climbs gradually, crossing a small streamlet, then turns westward as it begins to gain noticeable altitude. Eventually, it swings south as the trees become predominantly evergreen. After another long, shallow, diagonal climb back to the west, the trail emerges onto the Summit Glades ski trail (no sign). The narrow ski trail allows the first view past Deer Leap Rock, the Chittenden Reservoir, and on to some of the highest peaks in the Green Mountains.

Make a note of the intersection, which has only a blue blaze, not a sign, in case you decide to walk down the ski trail on your way back. After twenty paces, the Sherburne Trail reenters the woods on the left, marked again by only a blue blaze, no sign. At this point, you have a choice of taking the steeper ski trail or the flatter footpath to the summit. If you favor the woods, turn left. Continue almost a half mile along a relatively level section of trail. Just after a small spring, marked by a small white pipe poking out of the hillside, you will reach Pico Shelter at 2.5 miles.

Pico Shelter is an excellent place to sleep if you are backpacking. It has rough bunks, a table, and a superb view of Killington Peak. If you are planning an overnight, remember campfires are not allowed in the Coolidge

View of Pico Peak from the summit of Killington

Range (Killington and Pico region). Use the designated wash pit, not the water source, for cleaning yourself, your dog, and your dishes. The shelter operates on a first-come, first-served basis. A GMC Ridgerunner resides there from May through November and may collect a $5 overnight fee. If the shelter is full, you may not tent-camp by the shelter. The overflow camping area is 0.3 mile away on a nearby ski trail.

For the final 0.4-mile climb to the summit, turn right, passing the entrance to the shelter, onto the Pico Link Trail (blue blazes). The trail climbs steeply past the back of the shelter to another ski trail. Look left for a more expansive view of Killington Peak.

Cross the ski trail and reenter the woods by a small rock cairn. The trail continues to climb steeply to a gravel work road. Turn left, heading up the road for a short fifteen paces, then turn right, through a strip of trees onto yet another ski trail, called "Forty-Niner" (no sign). Turn left one last time, and walk up "Forty-Niner" toward the communication towers on the summit.

Just below the summit, the trail comes to the Warming Hut and the top of a chairlift. The Warming Hut is open year-round. The small deck on the front of the Warming Hut is the perfect picnic spot, with built-in benches around its railing. The views are spectacular of nearby Killington to the south and Ascutney, the pointed peak with ski trails, farther to the southeast. Look past the lift terminal to the north, where the layers of peaks include Mount Abraham, Mount Ellen, and even Mount Mansfield on clear day.

For a view to the west, you need to hike slightly farther to the true summit of the mountain. However, the summit is a jumble of work roads, maintenance buildings, lift terminals, and communication towers. It is worth a quick glance, but the Warming Hut offers the serenity that most dog lovers seek on a mountaintop. (Note: Keep your dog clear of the chairlifts at all times. The lifts can turn on at any time, even in summer.)

36. Pleiad Lake

Round trip: 0.8 mile
Hiking time: 1 hour
High point: 2150 feet
Elevation gain: 150 feet
Difficulty: 1 paw (easy)
Pet policy: None, but leash dogs out of the car; the trailhead is on a
   blind hill along a busy route
Map: USGS Bread Loaf Quad
Location: Bread Loaf, VT (between Ripton and Hancock)
Contact: Green Mountain National Forest–Middlebury District,
   802-388-4362, *www.fs.fed.us/r9/gmfl/*; Green Mountain Club,
   802-244-7037, *www.greenmountainclub.org*

Getting there: The trailhead is on Route 125 at the top of Middlebury Gap (just east of the Middlebury Snow Bowl), where the Long Trail crosses the road. The best parking is in the sizable turnout on the south side of the road. Take the Long Trail South (not North).

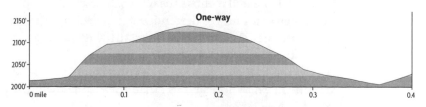

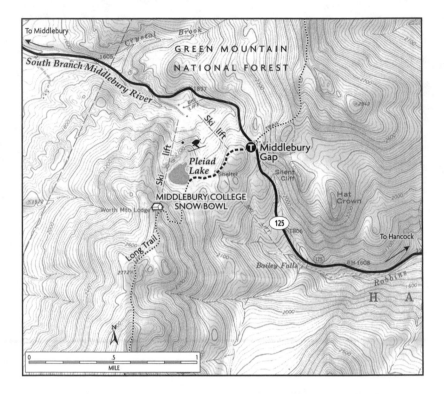

Located at the northern end of the Moosalamoo region on a shoulder of Worth Mountain, Pleiad Lake is one of the highest lakes in Vermont. A mere 0.4 mile from Route 125, it is surprisingly unknown among hikers, except for locals and those hiking the Long Trail (LT). This an excellent puppy hike, because there is little vertical and the terrain is smooth.

From the trailhead, take the LT South (white blazes) up a short rise to a sign-in box. Just after the box, the LT comes to one of the ski trails at the Middlebury Snow Bowl. Bear left up the trail, angling toward the top of the chairlift. The trail crosses behind the bull-wheel, where you find the only expansive mountain view on the entire hike, stretching all the way to the Adirondack High Peaks on a clear day.

From the lift terminal, the trail reenters the woods. It descends steeply down old log steps, then continues to descend, but more gently (almost flat) until it crosses another ski trail. From here, it traverses on good footing generally southward.

At about 0.3 mile the trail crosses a streamlet and comes to a fork. Bear right, leaving the LT on a short spur to Pleiad Lake (still downhill).

After crossing a third ski trail, the trail climbs slightly to the edge of the lake, a pond really. It is a peaceful spot. A loosely defined footpath skirts the right side of the lake, past a broad rock that is often used as an illegal tent site. It ends at another unofficial tent site.

The hike to Pleiad Lake is "inverted," meaning you hike down first. The lake will delight any dog. If you need to travel across the state of Vermont, it is worth taking Route 125, if only for this quick hike. But before Rover romps into the water, check that there are no beavers in the lake. You should not let your dog take a dip if beavers are swimming.

If you want more mileage, you can continue on the LT to several lookouts en route to the wooded summit of Worth Mountain (elevation 3234) at 2.7 miles. Please do not camp by the lake or on the slopes of the Middlebury Snow Bowl. Backpackers should stay at the Worth Mountain Lodge atop Worth Mountain, which is owned by Middlebury College and is open seasonally from May 1 to October 31.

Bravo cools off in Pleiad Lake.

37. Silver Lake

Round trip: 5.1 miles
Hiking time: 3.5 hours
High point: 1250 feet
Elevation gain: 630 feet
Difficulty: 2 paws (moderate)
Pet policy: Pets must be on leash around picnic area and campground
Map: USGS East Middlebury Quad
Location: East side of Lake Dunmore near Goshen, VT
Contact: Moosalamoo Association, 802-247-3971, *www.moosalamoo*
.org; Green Mountain National Forest–Middlebury District,
802-388-4362, *www.fs.fed.us/r9/gmfl/*

Getting there: On the east side of Lake Dunmore, follow Route 53 for 0.2 mile south of Branbury State Park. The best parking is at the main trailhead, the second one (farther south), on the east side of the road.

This hike is over 5 miles but gets a 2-paw (moderate) rating because the elevation gain is minimal. Silver Lake shares the same approach as Mount Moosalamoo for the first half mile, but after that it is an entirely different hiking experience taking you to a pristine lake with an interesting past.

From the parking lot, walk up a short rise to a Forest Service access road, an unpaved lane that is not open to motorized traffic. Turn right, heading up the road, which soon passes under a huge pipe called a penstock. The penstock feeds water from Silver Lake (elevation 1250) down to a local hydroelectric power station nearly 700 feet below on Route 53. Built in 1922, the station first provided power to the iron mines in Mineville, New York. Today it produces electricity for over 800 homes in the

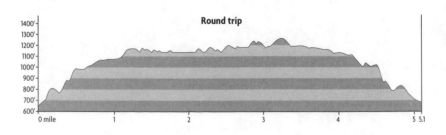

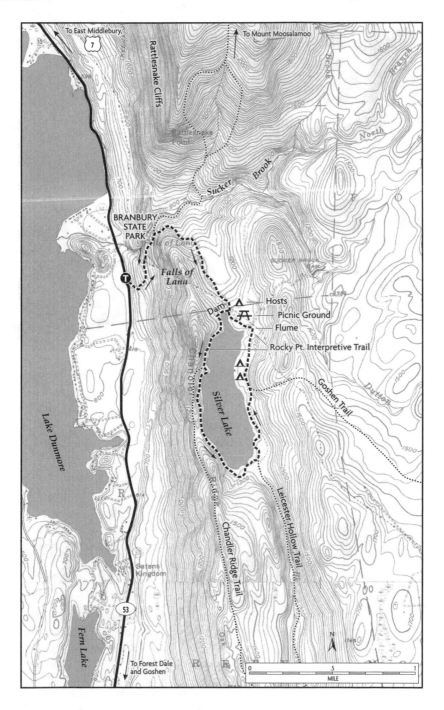

View of Mount Moosalamoo across Silver Lake

Moosalamoo area. But this seemingly industrial intrusion is completely hidden from you and your dog, except for the penstock.

At 0.5 mile the road passes the top of the Falls of Lana, an impressive waterfall fed by Sucker Brook, often a raging torrent. Use care if you hike down toward the falls for a better look—the roots are slick. This is NOT a good place for your dog to take a swim, so be sure to keep her on a leash.

From the top of the falls, the trail parallels Sucker Brook as it climbs gently to an intersection with the trail to Rattlesnake Cliffs and the summit of Mount Moosalamoo. Oddly, a public outhouse is in the center of the intersection. Turn right, continuing along the service road. As you climb, ignore the various side trails and roads that enter from the right.

At 1.6 miles the road reaches a grassy area at the northern tip of the lake. As you approach the lake, you must put your dog on a leash. She will want to swim at first sight of the water, but there are better, less populated spots.

The 2.5-mile trail around Silver Lake, called the Rocky Point Interpretive

Trail (blue blazes), is marked with eighteen points of interest. A booklet containing a map and an explanation of each numbered spot is available in a bin at the welcome sign.

Head right (west) over the small dam, which did not create the lake but enlarged it (the original lake was about 6 feet lower). Silver Lake has been a backcountry destination since the mid-1800s. In its prime, from 1880 to 1910, The Silver Lake Hotel, which stood where the picnic grounds are now, attracted up to 100 guests at a time. Today, only a few foundation stones remain.

Once past the dam, the trail becomes increasingly primitive but well marked.

About twenty minutes into the lake loop, the Chandler Ridge Trail enters from the right. The Chandler family lived at Silver Lake for about sixty years, starting in the 1870s. During that time, members of the family uncovered various tools and arrowheads left behind by the Abenakis. These artifacts eventually led archeologists to find two dugout canoes at the bottom of the lake, both over 600 years old.

As you round the south end of the lake, Mount Moosalamoo dominates the view across the water. This end of the lake is swampier and buggier, so bring some bug spray and be sure to squirt both yourself and your dog.

The footing becomes drier and smoother on the second half of the loop. At one point, the trail passes a glade of birches leading up to a piney point. From here the trail dips away from the lake, crosses a stream, then rises to an intersection with the Leicester Hollow Trail, which is more forest road than footpath. A little farther, the Goshen Trail enters from the right. This is a good place to put your dog on a leash. The path is wide, the footing is easy, and the campground (tent-camping only) is a short 0.3 mile away.

Just before completing the loop around the lake, the trail crosses a bridge over a flume. In 1916 the Hortonia Power Company, the predecessor to Central Vermont Public Service, built this concrete channel in order to divert water from Sucker Brook and Dutton Brook into Silver Lake and thus increase the volume of water flowing through its generators. Dogs and flumes are mutually exclusive. Your dog should already be on her leash at this point, but just in case....

Complete the loop around the lake by passing through the picnic area and by the campground hosts' campsite, then retrace your steps down the service road back to the parking lot.

UPPER CONNECTICUT RIVER VALLEY

38. Mount Ascutney

Round trip: 6.4 miles
Hiking time: 5 hours
High point: 3150 feet
Elevation gain: 2400 feet
Difficulty: 4 paws (strenuous)
Map: USGS Windsor Quad
Location: Brownsville, VT
Contact: Ascutney Trails Association, 802-674-9509

Getting there: From Windsor, take Route 44 toward Brownsville and the Ascutney Mountain Resort. The trailhead and parking area are on the left, about 4.5 miles west of Windsor.

A true monadnock, a singular peak that is not part of a ridge, Mount Ascutney stands alone in southeastern Vermont. It is one of the most recognizable landmarks in the region. The Abenakis called the mountain "Cas-cad-nac," which means, "mountain with the rocky summit." The

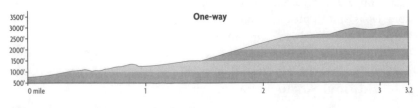

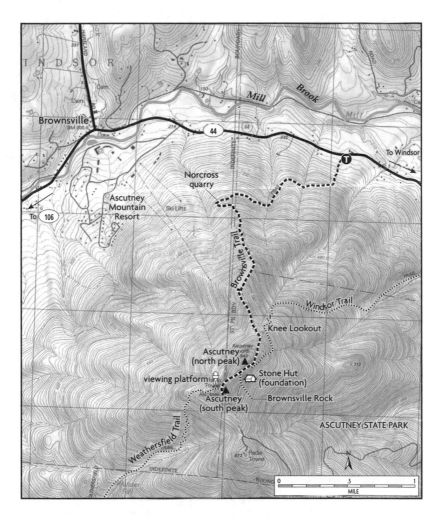

name is misleading. While there are areas of open rock around the summit, Ascutney does not have an open, bald top, but it is worth the hike for historic and scenic reasons.

There are four main hiking routes up the mountain. Cut in 1898, the Brownsville Trail (white blazes) is the second oldest, dog-friendly, and the most interesting with its climb through an old granite quarry. From the parking lot, the trail winds up through a strip of hardwoods between two hillside pastures. A stream flows to your right during wet periods, but like the rest of the trail, it is often dry. Do not forget to bring water for your dog.

Remains of the Stone Hut, the former fire-watcher's cabin on Mount Ascutney

The first section of trail is a heart-pounder until it meets an old woods road about a quarter mile from the trailhead. Turn right, heading up the road at a more moderate rate. At about 0.5 mile the trail crosses a stream with a high waterfall to your left. The waterfall is often reduced to a trickle, but it can be lovely during spring runoff or after a heavy rain.

At 1.1 miles the trail reaches the remains of the Norcross granite quarry. There are cables, enormous old pulleys, and large beams strewn around the site, not to mention huge granite blocks. Carefully climb over a few chunks of granite to catch a view to the north.

This is a good place to put your dog on a leash, unless you want him to take a dip in the old quarry hole, which is now an algae-infested pool.

From the quarry, the trail turns up sharply to the left on a footpath that cuts through the old quarry. The rocky walls are sheer, although now covered with ferns and trees, as if Mother Nature is slowly reclaiming the quarry for her own. There is a lookout from the top of the quarry across neighboring farmland. It is a pleasant spot and a destination for many hikers who do not care to reach the summit. For those who go on, the trail continues to climb steadily through a glade of towering evergreens. Watch the white blazes carefully in this area. The way is well marked, but there is hardly any undergrowth, so it is easy to lose the trail.

At 2 miles you reach Knee Lookout, with a view west across the Connecticut River Valley to Mount Kearsarge. A few steps later, the trail feels awash in green as ferns suddenly take over as the main undergrowth, a stark contrast to the relatively barren evergreen glade below.

The trail reaches a noticeable plateau and a stubby birch grove at 2.4 miles. This is the North Peak, elevation 2660 feet. The official "North Peak Vista" is a bit farther, offering views of Killington (straight ahead) and Okemo (slightly left). The main summit is still 0.8 mile away.

The trail sags, then heads up one last time through a birch and fern forest to the summit area. At 2.7 miles the Windsor Trail enters from the left. From here it is an easy stroll past the foundation of the Stone Hut, the former fire-watcher's cabin, and the short spur to Brownsville Rock, a well-known strategic lookout during Colonial times. Continue a short 0.2 mile to the site of the former fire tower, which was replaced by a lower, sturdier viewing platform in 1989.

39. Spruce Mountain

Round trip: 4.4 miles
Hiking time: 3 hours
High point: 3037 feet
Elevation gain: 1340 feet
Difficulty: 2 paws (moderate)
Map: USGS Knox Mountain Quad
Location: L. R. Jones State Forest; near Plainfield, VT
Contact: Vermont Department of Forests, Parks and Recreation,
  802-476-0184, *www.state.vt.us/anr*

Getting there: From Route 2 in the center of Plainfield, head south on Brook Road, which becomes Reservoir Road. If approaching from Route

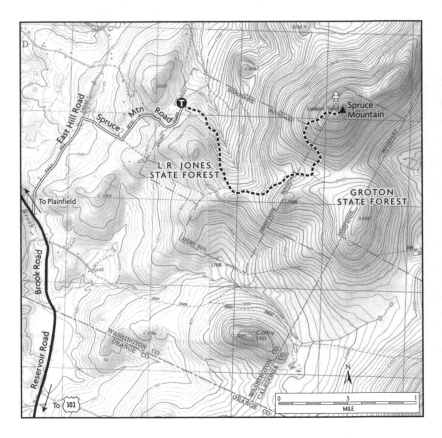

302, turn north onto Reservoir Road east of Orange. Turn onto East Hill Road. Turn right on Spruce Mountain Road. Bear left at the next junction and continue to the parking area and gate. Note: Trails are closed from April 15 to Memorial Day (mud season) to prevent trail damage.

Although the top of Spruce Mountain is in Groton State Forest, most of the peak is in L. R. Jones State Forest. In fact, the mountain is not accessible from Groton State Forest. The 642-acre L. R. Jones State Forest was the first parcel of land purchased by the State of Vermont, back in 1909. It is named for a former professor of botany at the University of Vermont in honor of his efforts to create a state tree nursery.

Spruce Mountain is the perfect hike for all but young pups and feeble senior dogs, although there are a couple of places where your dog will have to stretch up the side of a big rock. There are no ledges to scramble up, and it is a quiet route. The trail begins on an old logging road through a forest dominated by white and yellow birch. The blue blazes are intermittent at best, but the way is obvious, and the ascent is gentle.

After passing a couple of small clearings, the trail becomes a mosaic of large stepping stones. A small pool lies on the left, although it is not a great spot for a doggie dip, particularly later in the summer when it is likely to be filled with algae. After about a half hour the trail crosses a stream, a good spot for a break, although you will hardly feel fatigued. Pause for your dog to take a sip, though.

The logging road narrows into a regular footpath, which ascends through a corridor of spruce trees (no surprise!) and birches, then passes a large boulder on your right, which looks jailed behind a column of birch trees. A short rock wall lies around the bend, but there is no need to give your pooch a boost. He can easily find a way up the right side of the rock.

The trail crosses slabs of bedrock as you gain altitude, soon becoming steeper. Glimpses of the surrounding hills are seen through the trees. The corridor opens briefly in a small meadow of ferns before reentering the spruce trees and climbing along the summit ridge to the fire tower.

The original tower was built in 1919. The current tower dates back to 1944, but it has not been used since 1974. Today it is listed as a National Historic Lookout. It gives a vast 360-degree view, across miles of ponds and rolling hills to the north and south. Mount Mansfield and many of the highest peaks of the Green Mountains lie to the west. Mount Moosilauke, Franconia Ridge, and the Presidentials (on a clear day) in New Hampshire

A large boulder "jailed" behind a column of birches on Spruce Mountain

lie to the east. Do not allow your dog to climb the fire tower! The stone foundation of the former fire warden's cabin and a flat, open rock (the best picnic spot) lie just beyond the fire tower. This is the best spot to give your dog a bowl of water, a biscuit, and a belly rub.

40. Mount Tom and The Pogue

Round trip: Less than 1 mile to 5+ miles (depending on route)
Hiking time: 0.5–3.5 hours (depending on route)
High point: 1250 feet
Elevation gain: 550–900 feet (depending on route)
Difficulty: 1–2 paws (easy to moderate, depending on route)
Pet policy: Dogs need leashes in park at all times; in winter, no dogs on groomed snow trails; dogs not allowed in The Pogue
Maps: USGS Woodstock North Quad; park trail maps available at the park's Carriage Barn Visitor Center and at the Billings Farm & Museum
Location: Marsh-Billings-Rockefeller National Historical Park; Woodstock, VT
Contact: Billings Park Commission (Town of Woodstock), 802-457-4627; Marsh-Billings-Rockefeller National Historical Park, 802-457-3368, *www.nps.gov/mabi*

Getting there: From Route 4 in the middle of Woodstock, take Route 12 north. Just after crossing an iron bridge, turn left onto River Street. The trailhead is at the edge of a cemetery (an unmarked old carriage road). Best parking is next to the trailhead, or turn right shortly after the cemetery on Mountain Avenue and continue to Faulkner Park where the trail system is accessible from the Faulkner Trail. Alternate parking is available at the Billings Farm & Museum, located on Route 12 just past the turn onto River Street.

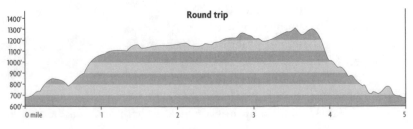

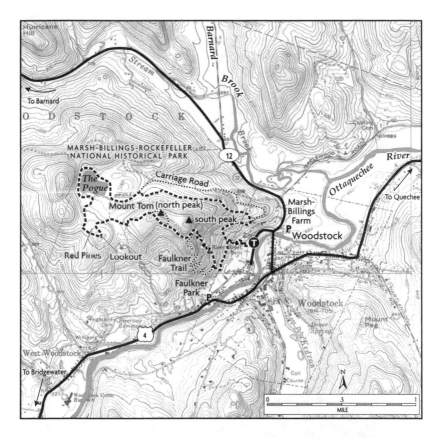

Formally known as a small ski area, Mount Tom is hardly a dominant peak in the state, yet it is a Vermont landmark for its historical significance.

Laurance S. Rockefeller was third in a series of pioneers in American land conservation and forest stewardship to own the Marsh-Billings estate, located at the base of Mount Tom. Generations of the Marsh and Billings families left a legacy of trails and carriage roads connecting the estate's many gardens and forest plantations. Rockefeller purchased the small ski area on Mount Tom's northeastern side, and owned other properties in Woodstock, including the Woodstock Inn, which he upgraded into a resort. In 1992, Rockefeller and his wife Mary, a Billings heir, gifted the mansion and the 550-acre forest behind it to the United States government. In 1998, the estate became the Marsh-Billings-Rockefeller National Historical Park, the only national park to focus on conservation history and land stewardship in America.

The designation "historical park" is important as dogs are generally not allowed on trails in regular national parks. The park's hiking trails connect seamlessly to the trail system on the summit and off the southeastern side of the mountain down to Faulkner Park, which is owned by the Town of Woodstock.

The hiking trails around Mount Tom are a maze, but if you carry a compass, you can take virtually any trail in the direction you want to go and eventually reach your destination.

The easiest and clearest way to reach the top is from Faulkner Park, up the Faulkner Trail. It is supposed to resemble the famous "Cardiac Trail" in Baden-Baden, Germany; however, anyone who is remotely fit will not experience much heart pounding. The hike is about as close to a proverbial "walk in the park" as you can take and still reach the top of a mountain in this state. It has no obvious blazes, but it is manicured, with periodic park benches on which to rest. With its long traverses, easy footing, and numerous switchbacks, the Faulkner Trail ascends almost without effort for most of the climb. It is a lovely walk through open glades. It turns more interesting just below the summit where you have to maneuver along the edge of a rocky cliff, which can be slippery when wet. A hand cable keeps you honest. The south peak is 1.6 miles and an easy hour from the car.

Hand cables aid the descent from Mount Tom toward Faulkner Park.

If you have more time and desire more mileage, it is worth saving the South Peak for last. Begin your hike on the North Peak Trail, which begins on the east side (right side) of the River Street Cemetery on a bridle path. Follow the bridle path past the "Billings Trails" sign.

Just over ten minutes into your hike, turn left on a footpath (no sign or blazes). The path makes your route more hike-like and simply parallels the carriage road. The path bends left, heading in a northwesterly direction toward The Pogue, a lovely mountain pond in the heart of the national historical park.

At about 0.7 mile, turn right at an obvious four-way intersection. After a short way, the trail meets the carriage road again and a grassy meadow, where Mount Ascutney is visible on a decent day. Turn left onto the carriage road to descend to The Pogue. Neither dogs nor their masters are allowed to swim in The Pogue. The bridle path makes a 0.8-mile loop around The Pogue, a must if you have walked this far for its tranquility and natural beauty. This entire hike would also make a good trail run if you are so inclined.

As you complete The Pogue loop, turn right onto a footpath that leads through a meadow, then along the edge of a large stand of red pine, one of the park's many historic forestry exhibits. Turn into the pines, then head up the gentle slope at every opportunity until you reach an open knoll with a bench. This lookout offers another excellent view of Mount Ascutney to the south. In the fall, the European larches (similar to tamaracks) turn the entire hillside on the left to gold. Continue on, descending back into the woods. Bear right at the fork onto a woods road, passing another overlook and continuing on to the south peak about a mile away. En route, you will pass a spur to the north peak, which is actually 109 feet higher than its sibling, but without a view.

A myriad of roads and trails converge on the south peak with its 180-degree view. There are two benches on the summit area. The smaller one looks westward toward the village of Bridgewater and Killington Peak, which is visible behind the nearer hills. The larger, semicircular bench gives a bird's-eye view of the Billings Farm & Museum lands to the left of the village of Woodstock.

From here, begin descending via the Faulkner Trail. At the intersection with the Upper Link Trail, go straight on the Upper Link. At the intersection with the Precipice Trail, turn right or you will end up back on the summit. At the next intersection, between the Precipice Trail and the Lower Link Trail, turn left, continuing on the Precipice Trail until it meets the original carriage road close to the trailhead.

NORTH-CENTRAL VERMONT

41. Burnt Rock Mountain

Round trip: 5.2 miles
Hiking time: 4 hours
High point: 3160 feet
Elevation gain: 2090 feet
Difficulty: 3 paws (ambitious)
Pet policy: Leash dogs on summit area to keep them off fragile sub-alpine vegetation
Map: USGS Huntington Quad
Location: North Fayston, Vermont
Contact: Green Mountain Club, 802-244-7037, *www.greenmountain club.org;* Vermont Department of Forests, Parks & Recreation, 802-879-6565, *www.state.vt.us/anr;* Mad River Glen Naturalist Program, 802-496-3551, *www.madriverglen.com*

Getting there: From Route 100 between Waitsfield and Duxbury, head west on the North Fayston Road, which turns to dirt. At 4 miles bear right at a fork, then immediately left (straight) at another fork onto Big Basin

One-way

3500'			
3000'			
2500'			
2000'			
1500'			
1000'			
0 mile	1	2	2.6

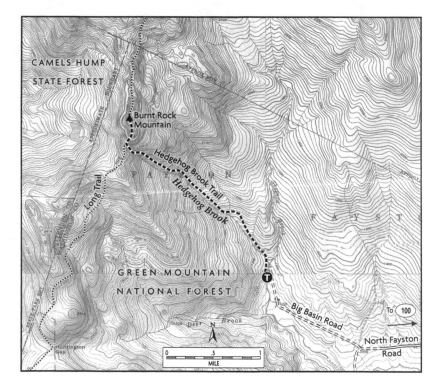

Road. The trailhead is on the left, about 1.5 miles from the second fork, just before the road ends at a private property sign. Do not drive or walk past this sign. There is parking on either side of the road by the trailhead.

Burnt Rock Mountain is an impressive rocky dome, located along the Long Trail just north of Huntington Gap. Its summit was cleared of trees in a forest fire about a century ago. Today, a few scrub spruce and fir dot the multiple ledges and humps of rock, having little impact on the 360-degree view but creating a number of private perches on the rare day other hikers are on the summit with you. Burnt Rock Mountain is not at the top of many hikers' lists outside the Mad River Valley. It should be, especially with a dog! When approached via the Hedgehog Brook Trail (blue blazes), it is a reasonable half-day outing and a shorter alternative to neighboring 4000-footers with equally spectacular views in all directions.

The Hedgehog Brook Trail immediately crosses its namesake brook upon leaving the parking lot. This can be a difficult or impossible crossing during spring runoff or after heavy rains, but otherwise it is not a

Kylee and Zoya on the summit of Burnt Rock Mountain

problem. From the opposite bank, the trail arcs to the right, away from the brook and begins to climb rather stiffly. It crosses a streamlet, then continues up through a hardwood forest. White ash is abundant, a sign that the soil here is rich.

At about 0.3 mile the trail begins a lengthy traverse to the northwest, descending gradually to an old woods road at 0.6 mile. Along the way, it crosses a couple of streams and an old logging trail. The trail takes an obvious turn to the left onto the woods road, as sticks and a sign bar the way to the right. A few minutes later, the trail passes a large boulder, capped with several sizable trees, then climbs at a moderate pitch along the right side of the brook. At about 0.8 mile the trail re-crosses the brook and narrows to a footpath, as it veers away from the water, climbing steadily.

By 1.1 miles, the trail passes under a substantial birch tree that collapsed over the trail, about ten feet overhead, probably a result of the severe region-wide ice storm in 1998. The increase in altitude starts to become evident as the trail now enters the lower edge of the boreal forest. Beyond the birch archway the trail bends to the southwest, and though the pitch eases, it becomes rougher and wetter. Watch for moose in this area and put your dog on a leash if he picks up an animal scent. Moose tracks in the mud are common.

At about 1.7 miles the trail crosses another stream, the last reliable water. A broad rock offers a nice spot for a rest while your dog gets refreshed in the small pools. From here, the trail arcs back in a more westerly direction and begins a steep push to a ridge on the upper shoulder of the mountain. The trail in this section is washed out in places and uses a short ladder to scale a rock slab. The ladder is more staircase than rungs. Your dog will likely ignore the ladder completely, opting instead to walk up the rock.

Above the ladder, the trail becomes more vertical and interesting, with scrambles up rocky outcroppings among the fir and spruce. At 2 miles the Hedgehog Brook Trail ends at the Long Trail (white blazes). Turn right (north), traversing mossy slab hemmed in by softwoods. Moments later, the trail crosses a muddy area where you can see the summit ahead.

At 2.3 miles, the trail hops off a boulder. It turns left through a cut in the rock, then right to begin its final ascent. After a small sag, it is a short but steep, gnarly climb to the summit ledges. The route passes several lookouts to the southeast toward the Sugarbush and Mad River ski areas. It bends left, squeezing between a tall rock face and a boulder, then breaks into the open. Follow the white blazes carefully on the upper mountain to find the route, which winds among the scrub trees and along the many rocky outcroppings.

The trail reaches the summit at 2.6 miles. Camels Hump is directly north beyond the Allen Range. The Worcester Mountains lie to the northeast. The White Mountains in New Hampshire are visible due east beyond the Mad River Valley on a clear day. The Monroe Skyline snakes to the south, and the High Peaks area of the Adirondacks in New York dot the western horizon.

42. Camels Hump

Round trip: 5.7 miles
Hiking time: 4.5 hours
High point: 4083 feet
Elevation gain: 1950 feet
Difficulty: 3 paws (ambitious)
Fees and permits: $5 overnight fee for use of the Montclair Glen
  Lodge
Pet policy: Dogs must be leashed above tree line and around
  Montclair Glen Lodge
Map: USGS Huntington Quad
Location: Huntington Center, VT
Contact: Vermont Department of Forests, Parks & Recreation,
  802-879-6565, *www.state.vt.us/anr;* Green Mountain Club,
  802-244-7037, *www.greenmountainclub.org*

Getting there: In Huntington Center, turn onto Taft Road. Turn onto
Camels Hump Road and follow the signs. Go past the first trailhead for
the Forest City Trail. Best starting point and parking are at the upper
parking lot.

Camels Hump is a Vermont landmark, a bald peak with a distinct shape.
In the late 1700s the mountain was dubbed "Camels Rump" by Ira Allen
(Ethan Allen's brother), which was later changed to the more socially
acceptable "Camels Hump." The Hump is sizable in looks and in effort,
but well worth the challenge. It is a popular climb, so save this one for
midweek, especially with a dog. The summit has a noisy reputation on
weekends and holidays due to barking dogs and occasional dog fights,
but midweek you may have the only pooch on the peak.

The mountain can be approached from both Duxbury and Huntington. The Huntington side is described here because you can make a
loop, ascending via the Forest City Trail and descending via the Burrows

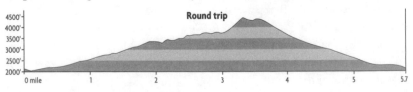

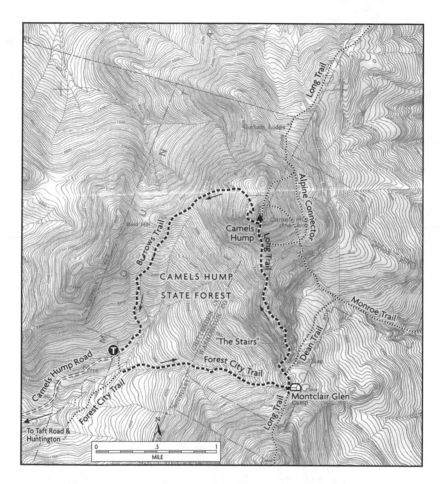

Trail. The Forest City Trail is a half mile longer than the Burrows Trail, with some interesting terrain that is easier to go up than to come down, and it offers numerous views of the summit during the last third of the climb.

From the trailhead, take the short connector over a bridge to the Forest City Trail (blue blazes). At the intersection with the Forest City Trail, turn left. The sizable stream will remain on your right for awhile as you climb steadily through a maple forest, which changes to birch and then to beech as you gain elevation.

Because of its distinct ecological zones that continue to all the way to the summit, Camels Hump is the site of ongoing environmental studies on the impact of acid rain and other related research. In 1965 the National Park Service named the mountain a National Natural

Leo leads the way across the saddle below the summit of Camels Hump.

Landmark. Research on Camels Hump played an instrumental role in linking the effects of pollutants from the Midwest to deforestation in New England, which ultimately contributed to the creation of the Clean Air Act.

The Forest City Trail reaches the Long Trail (LT) at 1.3 miles. Backpackers can sleep at the Montclair Glen Lodge, a small cabin built in 1948, located 200 feet to the right. The short trail to the cabin crosses a reliable brook, a good place for your dog to cool off. The cabin is available on a first-come, first-served basis. Dogs must be leashed around the lodge and dog waste must be properly managed by the animal's owner. There is a GMC Backcountry Caretaker in residence from May through November who will collect the $5 overnight fee.

Turn left on the LT (white blazes), heading north toward the summit. At the next intersection, with the Dean Trail and the Allis Trail, turn left, continuing on the LT North. The trail becomes noticeably steeper and rockier as you start to see the neighboring ridge—the Allen Range—to the right.

Things get interesting as the trail ascends the first of three "stairs," a rocky outcropping with the first real view. From the third "stair" you will get your first view of the Hump, which seems surprisingly far away. The "stairs" can be intimidating for novice hikers, but dogs seem to find their way up the rocky crags without much difficulty. Allow them to go off-leash, keeping them nearby with verbal commands through this section.

After the "stairs," the trail dips into a saddle as it approaches the final ascent. You will have frequent views of the Hump, like an imposing wall looming ahead through breaks in the low evergreen canopy. At 0.2 mile from the summit, the Long Trail meets the Alpine Trail, a connector to the Monroe Trail from the Duxbury side of the mountain and a bypass of the summit if the weather is bad.

From this point on, you are in a fragile alpine zone above tree line. Dogs must be on a leash. Both you and your dog should walk only on the designated trail. The summit of Camels Hump is one of only three areas of alpine vegetation in Vermont. A number of the plants here are on the endangered species list. What look like grassy fields and green patches among the rocks are extremely sensitive areas. Once on the summit, stay on the rocks to pick your lunch spot.

The 360-degree view from the summit is phenomenal. On a clear day, you can see west across the Champlain Valley to the Adirondacks, east to the White Mountains, and north and south along the Green Mountain Range.

To descend via the Burrows Trail, continue on the LT North (do not retrace your steps). At 0.3 mile below the summit, you will reach a clearing and a three-way intersection. This was the site of a former guest house, a popular destination during the Civil War; however, its popularity diminished with the development of Mount Mansfield and the Stowe area. At the clearing, turn left onto the Burrows Trail (blue blazes) and descend the remaining 2.4 miles to the parking lot.

43. Mount Elmore

Round trip: 2.4 miles (fire tower); 3.4 miles (Balanced Rock)
Hiking time: 2.5 hours (fire tower); 3.5 hours (Balanced Rock)
High point: 2608 feet
Elevation gain: 1450 feet
Difficulty: 2 paws (moderate)
Fees and permits: $2.50 age 14 and over; $2 children ages 4–13
Pet policy: Carry proof of current rabies vaccination; no dogs at lake area; leash 10 feet or less
Map: USGS Hyde Park Quad
Location: Elmore State Park; Morrisville, VT
Contact: Vermont Department of Forests, Parks & Recreation, 802-476-0184, www.vtstateparks.com; Green Mountain Club, 802-244-7037, www.greenmountainclub.org

Getting there: Take Route 12 to Elmore State Park. From the tollbooth, continue straight ahead to the trailhead. There is a cabin with a picnic

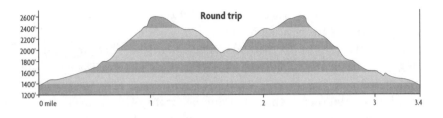

table to the right in the woods near the parking area. From the parking area, take the Fire Tower Trail (not the Nature Trail).

Mount Elmore is the lowest peak of the Worcester Range, but one of the more prominent (and more hiked) due to its position at the northern end of the range and its fire tower on top.

Fire tower on the upper ridge of Mount Elmore, in the distance, beyond the old stone work of the fire-watcher's cabin

From the parking area, the trail heads uphill on a fire road. If the gate is closed, walk around it, passing a stone chimney on the left in the woods. A few minutes later, the Beaver Pond Trail exits to the right. At 0.5 mile, at the end of the fire road, the Catamount Trail continues straight ahead. Take a sharp right, heading uphill on the Mount Elmore Trail (blue blazes).

The Mount Elmore Trail is a wide footpath that parallels a brook at first. The grade is fairly steep, but smooth. The incline eases somewhat as the trail swings sharply right, then continues climbing up stone steps. From there, it winds up the hillside, gaining altitude in waves.

At 1 mile the trail crosses bits of wet slab before reaching the spur to a lookout on the left. The lookout is also the site of the old fire watcher's cabin. The view, mainly to the east over Lake Elmore, stretches as far as Mount Washington. If hiking with an older or less agile dog, this is a good place to have a picnic and turn around.

To continue to the fire tower, return to the main trail, climbing on more rugged, vertical footing. Let your dog find her own way through this short section, off her leash, so you do not pull each other off balance. After the short scramble, the trail levels off, arriving at a T. Turn left and go only a few paces to reach the fire tower.

The fire tower is exceptionally tall, and worth the climb. (Leave your dog at ground level.) The view is phenomenal considering the short hike, with the Mount Mansfield ridge dominating to the west. Jay Peak and several peaks in southern Quebec fill the northern horizon. The Presidential Range, Franconia Ridge, and Mount Moosilauke poke up along the eastern skyline. The Worcester Range and main spine of the Green Mountains lie to the south.

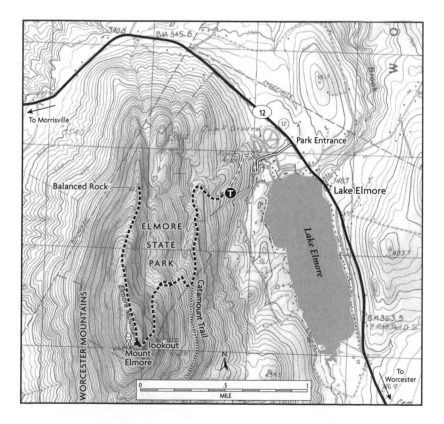

To continue to Balanced Rock, return to the T and head in the other direction. The extra hike over to Balanced Rock is worth the effort if you have the time, mainly for the oddity of it. Balanced Rock is a glacial erratic about twenty feet long and about six feet high, perched at an angle on a rocky outcropping. As the name implies, it seems to defy gravity. From the tower, the trail to Balanced Rock is flat and then downhill. It passes two lookouts, the first to Mount Mansfield and the second to Lake Elmore.

Years ago, the trail traveled past Balanced Rock, making a loop back to the Mount Elmore Trail, but today the loop peters out just below the cliff line. To return to the car, retrace your steps back to the T near the fire tower and down the Mount Elmore Trail.

44. Mount Hunger

Round trip: 4.4 miles
Hiking time: 3.5 hours
High point: 3538 feet
Elevation gain: 2290 feet
Difficulty: 4 paws (strenuous)
Map: USGS Stowe Quad
Location: C. C. Putnam State Forest; Waterbury Center, VT
Contact: Vermont Department of Forests, Parks & Recreation, 802-879-6565, *www.state.vt.us/anr;* Green Mountain Club, 802-244-7037, *www.greenmountainclub.org*

Getting there: From Route 100 in Waterbury Center, turn right onto Howard Avenue. Turn left on Maple Street at the far end of the small village green. Turn right on Loomis Hill, and travel uphill approximately 2 miles. At the crest of the hill, the road turns to dirt and bends left, becoming Sweet Road. Continue another 1.5 miles to the parking lot and trailhead on the right.

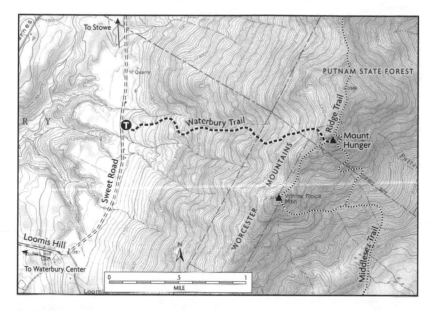

When polling frequent hikers in the Stowe area, the unanimous "must do" hike is Mount Hunger, one of the primary peaks in the Worcester Range, because it is relatively short but with a dazzling view. It is also a fun hike because the upper half of the climb has many boulders and ledges to scramble up. It is definitely one of the best day hikes in Vermont for humans, and it is okay for dogs, provided your dog is energetic and agile. Save this one for midweek to avoid other people and pets.

There are several ways to approach the summit of Mount Hunger, depending on how far you want to walk and whether you want to drop a car at another trailhead. The Waterbury Trail (blue blazes) is both the shortest and the most vertical route. It starts out in an open wood, strewn with mossy boulders. The footing is excellent, with many rock steps laid into the path thanks to the Vermont Youth Conservation Corp. The trail climbs moderately at first, with intermittent flat sections.

There might be a number of stream crossings if the weather has been wet, but most dry up without consistent rain, except for a rocky cascade at 1.1 miles. The trail crosses the stream, then turns left, following the left bank. Over the next rise, the trail bears right across the stream between the upper and lower portions of the falls. The waterfall is often no more than a trickle, but there is always some water in the pool to the left of the crossing where your dog can take a quick dip. From here the trail becomes progressively rockier and steeper. There is a brief reprieve through a patch of ferns and hobblebushes, a native shrub with broad leaves and large clusters of white flowers in mid-spring, then showy red berries by summer (not edible).

The trail continues through a birch grove that was stunted during the

A hiker breaks out of the trees on Mount Hunger.

severe ice storm of 1998, creating a break in the forest canopy. The first of several short rock walls is just around the bend. Guide your dog up the obvious diagonal crack, which functions like a narrow walkway. At 2 miles, the side trail to White Rock enters from the right. From here it is a short scramble to the summit.

The summit is bare rock with a 360-degree view, but it is tough to take your eyes off Mount Mansfield and Camels Hump, which dominate the skyline to the east beyond the Waterbury Reservoir. While not a true alpine zone—it is considered sub-alpine—take care that you and your pet stay on the bedrock and off the fragile vegetation. The Green Mountain Club recommends that you keep your dog on a leash on areas of the mountain above the trees.

For more variety and mileage, continue north along the Worcester Ridge to Stowe Pinnacle, 3.4 miles away, or farther to Mount Worcester, 5.2 miles away—although both of these options are typically hiked by leaving a car at the trailhead below either of those peaks rather than retracing your steps.

45. Lincoln Gap–Appalachian Gap

Total distance: 11.6 miles
Hiking time: 7 hours
High point: 4006 feet (Mount Abraham)
Elevation gain: 2520 feet
Difficulty: 4 paws (strenuous)
Fees and permits: $5 for overnight use of Battell Shelter
Pet policy: Leash pets on Mount Abraham summit to protect fragile alpine plants
Maps: USGS Lincoln Quad; USGS Mount Ellen Quad
Location: Warren, VT
Contact: Green Mountain Club, 802-244-7037, *www.greenmountain club.org;* Mad River Glen Naturalist Program, 802-496-3551, *www.madriverglen.com*

Getting there, Appalachian Gap trailhead (end of hike): From Route 100 in Waitsfield, take Route 17 west to the top of Appalachian Gap. The trailhead is on the left, on the south side of the gap. Leave a car in the parking area on the north side of the road. (**Alternate trailhead, Mad River Glen:** From Route 100 in Waitsfield, take Route 17 west to the Mad River Glen ski area. Park at the base lodge, which is on the left, about 2 miles below the top of Appalachian Gap.)

To Lincoln Gap trailhead (recommended start): From Route 100 in Warren, take Lincoln Gap Road west toward Lincoln. This is a narrow, steep road that is closed in the winter. The trailhead is at the top of the gap. Park on either side of the road.

This hike is a peak-bagger's dream, crossing at least four summits—Mount Abraham (elevation 4006 feet), Lincoln Peak (elevation 3972 feet), Mount Ellen (elevation 4083 feet), and General Stark Mountain (elevation 3662 feet)—depending on how you count them. Some maps also recognize Nancy Hanks Peak on the north side of Lincoln Peak and Cutts Peak on the south side of Mount Ellen, which would give you six summits in one trip. Others consider the entire ridge to be only two peaks—Lincoln and Stark—with prominent points like Mount Abraham to be part of the other two. Regardless of how you count them, this is one of the classic ridge-walks in Vermont, and a dog's delight, except for the last section between the top of General Stark and Appalachian Gap. For this reason, ending your hike down a ski trail at Mad River Glen is recommended if you are hiking with a smaller or less agile dog.

Otherwise, the descent to Appalachian Gap is an interesting final leg of the hike, with views and some challenges, including two short ladders. The ladders are the main reason why this hike is best done from south to north with a dog. It is easier for a dog to go down the two ladder pitches than to go up them. In addition, it is nice to get an early reward, reaching the summit of Mount Abraham, then to have a long, gradual descent most of the way from there.

The hike is on a section of the Long Trail (LT, white blazes) commonly called the Monroe Skyline, in honor of Will Monroe, who played a key role in locating it here. While the vertical gain is modest considering the route includes two of Vermont's five 4000-footers, the

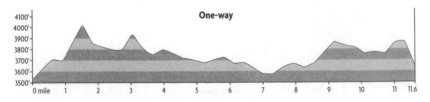

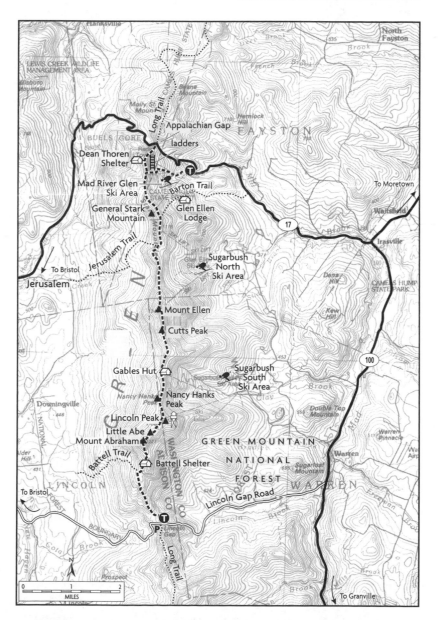

mileage makes it formidable as a day hike for all but the fittest dogs and their masters.

From the trailhead at Lincoln Gap, take the LT north. The trail is flat at first, then dips through a depression as it meanders through the woods on the approach to Mount Abraham. After about fifteen minutes, the trail starts climbing, becoming more rocky and rooted but nothing extreme. Periodic stone steps aid your footing. The trail winds up through a boreal forest, with glimpses to the west through the trees.

After crossing two streams, the trail reaches the intersection with the Battell Trail, another common route up Mount Abraham, at 1.7 miles. Bear right, continuing on the LT north to the Battell Shelter at 1.8 miles. Both the trail and the shelter are named for Joseph Battell, a conservationist and former owner of the Bread Loaf Inn, who cut a trail to Mount Ellen in 1901. The shelter is a simple lean-to with a picnic table, but it is a popular spot for backpackers who get a late start. The Green Mountain Club charges $5 per person per night. Campfires are not allowed.

Turn left (north) at the Battell Shelter to continue to the summit of Mount Abraham. Soon the trees get noticeably shorter, and the trail turns to slab. The ascent is steeper here, with views to the northwest. Then the trail flattens briefly, affording a view to the south.

Just below the summit, as the trail passes through scrub pines, there is a large, white quartzite rock on the left that looks like a giant egg. This is a good place to put your dog on a leash, as you are almost to the top of Mount Abraham where fragile alpine vegetation survives despite an abbreviated two-month growing season. The grass on the summit is mainly Bigelow's sedge. It looks like common grass, but it is only found on three summits in Vermont—Mount Mansfield, Camels Hump, and here. The alpine zone on Mount Abraham is the smallest of the three peaks, about the size of a large living room.

At 2.6 miles the trail reaches the summit, with its 360-degree panorama. The White Mountains dominate the eastern skyline. To the west you can see the Bristol Cliffs, Lake Champlain, and the Adirondacks in the distance. To the south, you can see down the spine of the Green Mountains as far as Killington. And Mount Mansfield pokes out from the east shoulder of Mount Ellen to the north.

From the top of Mount Abraham, bear right on the LT, reentering the woods. The ridge is not above tree line, which gives you a modicum of protection from the wind. The trail sags through a muddy area as it traverses the top of Little Abe (elevation 3900 feet), noticeable only because of the sign.

At 4.2 miles, the trail breaks out of the trees at the summit of Lincoln Peak, which is the top of the Sugarbush South ski area. There is a platform on the right, offering excellent views in all directions.

Descend to an open area, staying to the left. For the rest of this hike, which crosses several other ski areas, always stay left to keep the ridge. From here, the LT heads down into some spruce trees just past a small fire pit. It becomes narrower, with views to the west as you progress toward Mount Ellen first on a long, steady descent, then gently up again.

After passing a rock perch, the trail drops a bit more, then flattens out. The trail continues to roll along the ridge like a series of shallow waves, soon reaching the top of Sugarbush's Castle Rock chairlift. Turn left on the Middle Earth ski trail to continue on the LT, or take a break at the Gables warming hut, which is usually open and has a great view from its deck to the southeast across the Mad River Valley.

About 150 yards from Castle Rock, 4.8 miles from the trailhead, the LT turns left off the Middle Earth ski trail through Holt Hollow. A water source is about 200 feet down a spur trail to the left. As with any ridge-walk, this hike is relatively dry, so be sure to bring extra water for you and your dog, particularly on a hot day.

The trail ambles along, reaching the top of Mount Ellen at 6.3 miles. Mount Ellen is home to the Sugarbush North ski area. Again, stay left to keep the ridge, heading a short distance down a ski trail before reentering the woods just above a high wooden snow fence. A view to the northeast, with farmland below and hills beyond, lies before you. Descend through a steep, rocky area, crossing some scree before reentering the woods. From here the descent becomes steadier and gentler, periodically leaving the apex of the ridge to avoid blowdowns.

At 8.1 miles the Jerusalem Trail enters from the left. A few yards later, an overlook to the left (west) offers a nice place to pause before the last third of the hike. If you need water or a longer respite, continue a short way to the next intersection, with the Barton Trail, which leaves the ridge to the right. The Glen Ellen Lodge is only 0.3 mile down the Barton Trail. It has a reliable water source except during periods of drought.

From the junction with the Barton Trail, the LT ascends through a washed-out area, then climbs steadily for a short stretch toward the top of General Stark Mountain, a nondescript wooded hump. It levels off through a muddy area before reaching yet another ski trail, this time part of the Mad River Glen ski area and denoted by an orange disc high on a tree (to ensure it is above snow level in the winter). A short time later, the trail emerges onto a work road at 10.2 miles.

If you left your car at the Mad River Glen ski area, turn right and walk about 1 mile down the work road to the base of the ski area.

If you left your car at the top of Appalachian Gap, turn left up the road toward the antique lift tower. As you pass the lift, notice the old single chairlift, one of the oldest chairlifts in the United States. The LT goes behind the warming hut. There is an excellent view to the east from the deck of the hut.

Turn left just after the hut down the LT, not the ski trail that opens before you. The LT briefly breaks out along the edge of this ski trail below its first pitch, then it reenters the woods. In the winter, this section of the LT, called Paradise Glade, is skiable. At the fork, bear left to avoid descending a ski trail to the bottom of the ski area.

At this point, the trail begins its final descent to Appalachian Gap. It is steep, rocky, and washed out in sections. At one particularly sheer boulder, a short ladder assists humans. Dogs can easily go around it.

At 10.4 miles the LT passes the Theron Dean Shelter, a lean-to tucked into the trees on the left. Theron Dean was a friend of Will Monroe and an active member of the Green Mountain Club during its early years. There is no water at this shelter, but it is worth a visit. The view to the north into the gap from the cliffy perch is not for those afraid of heights.

Jason and Bravo take a break by the entrance of Dean's Cave.

A few steps farther on the left, a short spur goes through Dean's Cave, a narrow rock passageway, and loops back up to the shelter.

After passing the top of another ski lift, the trail reenters the woods for good. There is one more short ladder before reaching Appalachian Gap. Again, athletic, agile, mountain-savvy dogs, particularly bigger dogs like Labs, can negotiate the short, rocky face beside the ladder. Normally, hikes with ladders are not dog-friendly, but this one is an exception. The ladders are short and more for convenience than necessity.

46. Mount Mansfield

Round trip: 6.8 miles from parking area (including 0.2 mile to Cantilever Rock)

Hiking time: 5 hours

High point: 4393 feet

Elevation gain: 2550 feet

Difficulty: 4 paws (strenuous)

Fees and permits: $2.50 day-use fee

Pet policy, park campground: Pets must be attended at all times and on leashes of 10 feet or less in campgrounds. Proof of rabies vaccination is required for admission; puppies too young for vaccination will not be admitted. Clean up after your dog; pets must be kept quiet.

Pet policy, trail and summit area: Dogs may be off leash above the campground and below the alpine vegetation zone; above tree line, pets must be on leash of five feet or less.

Map: USGS Mount Mansfield Quad

Location: Underhill State Park; Underhill, VT

Contact: Underhill State Park, mid-May to mid-October, 802-899-3022; Vermont Department of Forests, Parks & Recreation, 802-879-6565 (off-season), *www.vtstateparks.com;* Green Mountain Club, 802-244-7037, *www.greenmountainclub.org*

Getting there: Take Route 15 to Underhill Flats. Turn east onto River Road, which bends to the left and becomes Pleasant Valley Road in Underhill Center. Turn right on Mountain Road which ends at Underhill State Park. The trailhead is technically a mile up the dirt road from the far end of the parking lot, but this is the farthest you can drive.

Just the fact that Mount Mansfield is the tallest peak in Vermont makes it a magnet for hikers. About 40,000 people make it to the top of this landmark each year, so it is wisest to take your turn midweek, especially if you are hiking with a dog.

Viewed from the east or west, the profile of the 2-mile summit ridge resembles the face of a man looking skyward. The prominent points of the ridge are commonly known from south to north as The Forehead, The Nose, The Upper Lip, The Lower Lip, The Chin, and Adam's Apple. The Chin, at 4393 feet, is the true summit.

The Sunset Ridge Trail (blue blazes) is a popular route to The Chin, because much of it is above tree line. It is among the easier routes for a dog, although there are several challenging sections. It also has a unique side attraction, called Cantilever Rock, a huge, narrow boulder that extends twenty-five feet from a cliff, parallel to the ground, seeming to defy gravity.

Begin in Underhill State Park, which lies within the 34,000-acre Mount Mansfield State Forest. The lower park around the ranger station has eleven tent sites, six lean-tos, and rest rooms with cold water and flush toilets, but no showers. RVs and tent-trailers are not recommended because the campsites are not immediately next to the parking lot.

Head up the dirt road at the end of the parking lot. The road is closed to traffic, but if you prefer a more trail-like path, take the Eagles Cut Trail (blue blazes), which starts at the upper parking lot. Both the road and the trail lead to the Sunset Ridge Trail, crisscrossing each other, until the trail merges with the road at 0.3 mile. At this point, you have no choice but to walk on the road. (Note: Your dog must be on a leash that is no longer than ten feet in the campground area, which is technically the entire first mile.)

When you reach the sign-in box at 1 mile, you have reached the Sunset Ridge Trail. Bear left into the woods, immediately crossing over three bridges before coming to the intersection with the Laura Cowles Trail at 1.1 miles. Bear left over another bridge to stay on the Sunset Ridge Trail. After a couple more bridges, the trail finally starts to climb over slab, scattered rocks, and rock steps, passing over even more bridges and by a large boulder.

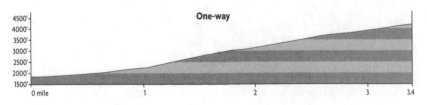

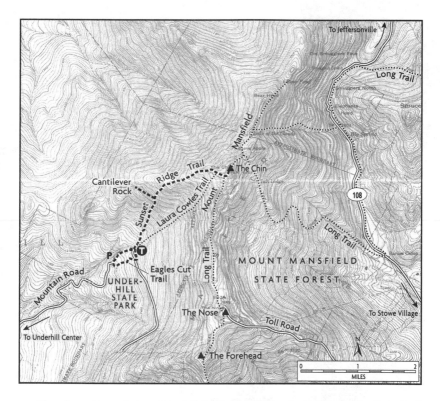

About an hour into your hike, you will come to the first of several steeper slabs. Humans tend to have an easier time going up the center crack, while dogs prefer the side of the rock. From the top of it, turn around for your first view of Camels Hump in the distance.

At 1.8 miles, the spur to Cantilever Rock departs to the left, only 0.1 mile away. It is worth the short side trip.

From here the Sunset Ridge Trail continues up through ferns and birches. It passes a chasm between three large boulders that were likely one boulder long ago. A few minutes later, the trail reaches another boulder formation, this time a small cave. You can walk through it, or go around on the main trail to keep your feet dry.

Several small overhangs will catch your eye as the trail winds up through the rock, then breaks out on a rocky outcropping. Technically, the alpine zone begins here. Please stop to put your dog on her leash. Sunset Ridge and The Chin tower above you to the left (northeast). Camels Hump dominates the view to the right (south). The Champlain Valley spreads out before you to the west.

Cantilever Rock on Mount Mansfield

Continue up the steep slab, where your dog will likely have an easier time than you will. One vertical spot may present a problem for smaller dogs, but larger breeds, like retrievers, should be fine. For the rest of the route, the vistas are endless, but it is tough to take your eyes off The Chin, the distinct rocky knob that looms above. First blueberries and then wild cranberries, also called lingonberries, carpet the rocks between the scrub spruce trees.

At the sign for the Chin Natural Area, the trail bends to the right, traversing toward The Nose. At the intersection with the upper end of the Laura Cowles Trail, bear left (up). At 3.2 miles the Sunset Ridge Trail ends at the summit ridge where it meets the Long Trail (LT). Turn left on the LT north over the duckboards (also called "bog bridges" or "puncheons"). Please keep your dog at heel and on the trail. (Hopefully, she has been on her leash since you cleared the tree line.) The remaining stretch to the summit can be crowded, and the rare plant species might not withstand trampling.

The stunted shrubs, sedges (grass-like plants), and lichens near the summit are more common to the Arctic tundra a thousand miles north. Scientists believe when the ice age retreated about 12,000 years ago these small alpine plants were more widespread, growing wherever the ice recently melted, but most died as the climate warmed. Today, only three peaks in Vermont support this type of plant life: Mount Mansfield, Camels Hump, and Mount Abraham. Mount Mansfield has the most expansive area of alpine vegetation; however, the plants are genetically isolated, extremely fragile, and slow-growing due to the harsh climate and thin soil. From May through November, Summit Caretakers from the Green Mountain Club are usually stationed at the top to educate hikers about the area's natural history, the alpine vegetation, and Leave No Trace ethics.

The advantage of being on the highest peak in Vermont is the expansive, unobstructed view in all directions. On a clear day, you can see all the way to Mount Royal in Montreal to the north, Whiteface Mountain and the Adirondacks across Lake Champlain to the west, Camels Hump and the main spine of the Green Mountains to the south, and the Worcester Range (close) and the White Mountains (far) to the east.

47. Stowe Pinnacle

Round trip: 3.2 miles
Hiking time: 2.5 hours
High point: 2740 feet
Elevation gain: 1520 feet
Difficulty: 2 paws (moderate)
Map: USGS Stowe Quad
Location: C. C. Putnam State Forest; Stowe, VT
Contact: Green Mountain Club, 802-244-7037, *www.greenmountain club.org;* Vermont Department of Forests, Parks & Recreation, 802-879-6565, *www.state.vt.us/anr*

Getting there: From the center of Stowe village, turn onto School Street. Bear right onto Stowe Hollow Road, which becomes Upper Hollow Road. The trailhead and parking area are just beyond Pinnacle Road, on the left. Note: Trails are closed from April 15 to Memorial Day (mud season) to prevent trail damage.

Stowe Pinnacle gives a big reward for a relatively small effort. It is a favorite among Stowe locals, with and without dogs. It is best to go midweek,

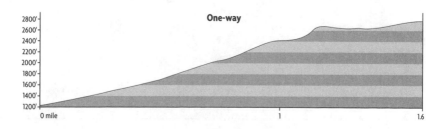

especially if your dog does not have impeccable social skills. Located in C. C. Putnam State Forest, the trail is an excellent half-day hike. Although there is not much water on the route, most of the hike is shaded, which makes it a good choice on a warm day.

The Stowe Pinnacle Trail (blue blazes) begins at the back of the parking lot through a meadow of wildflowers, heading directly at the mountain. The trail turns muddy as it approaches the woods, crossing a number of duckboards.

At about 0.3 mile the trail passes a giant rock cairn on top of a small boulder. It is a tradition for all who pass to add a stone to the cairn. The trail is wide and rock-strewn, so it is not a problem to find one. After the cairn, the trail becomes fairly steep until it reaches a bend to the left. From there, it traverses past a teepee made of saplings, then bends right and climbs again.

At 0.8 mile the trail continues through a couple of switchbacks, up muddy stone steps, a welcome aid on the sustained climb. At the top of the first series of steps, the path turns to step-like slab, then back to more real steps. The pattern continues, climbing steeply, until the trail reaches a height of land and a spur to the left leading to a worthwhile lookout. You can see the entire Mount Mansfield ridge to the west, Waterbury Reservoir and Sugarbush to the south (far left), and the village of Stowe to the north (right).

The pitch eases above the vista, as the trail bends right, at first descending, then angling up across a rooted side-hill. It steepens again for a short

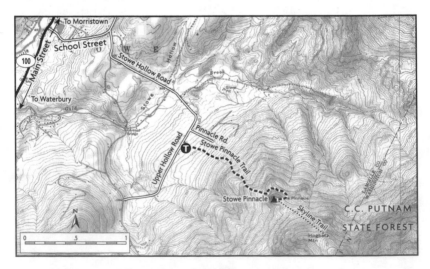

Fudge and Casper atop Stowe Pinnacle

way as it circles the mountaintop. At 1.4 miles you reach the junction with the Skyline Trail on the left, which crosses the Worcester Range to Mount Hunger. Bear right, climbing through a pine grove, then cross a long stretch of slab framed by scrub trees, reaching the summit at 1.6 miles.

Stowe Pinnacle is accurately named. Its summit is literally a pinnacle of bedrock, giving a 360-degree view. The long views past Mount Elmore to the north, Mount Mansfield to the west, and Sugarbush to the south are sure to impress you. The view to the east is less expansive, blocked by the wooded Worcester Ridge.

CHAMPLAIN VALLEY

48. Mount Independence

Round trip: 3.5 miles
Hiking time: 2.5 hours
High point: 306 feet
Elevation gain: 200 feet
Difficulty: 1 paw (easy)
Fees and permits: $5 day-use fee (pay inside visitor center); children 14 and under free
Pet policy: Dogs should be on leash
Map: USGS Ticonderoga Quad
Location: Orwell, VT
Contact: State of Vermont, Division for Historic Preservation, 802-759-2412; *www.historicvermont.org/mountindependence*

Getting there: From Orwell, take Route 78 west. Bear left onto Mount Independence Road, which turns to gravel, and follow it up a steep hill to the visitor center and parking area. The trailhead is above the visitor center. Note: Park hours are from 9:00 AM to 5:00 PM, Memorial Day through mid-October.

Mount Independence is a state historic site. It is unusual from a hiker's perspective because its trails wander through the ruins of a strategic

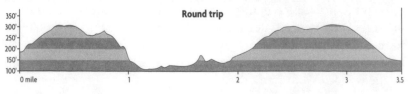

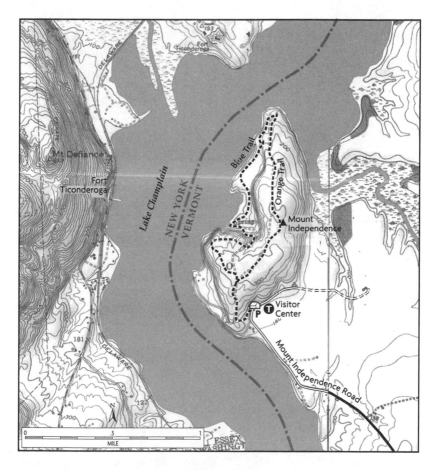

American stronghold that dates back to the Revolutionary War, and because it is one of the few real hikes along the shores of Lake Champlain, though not exactly a wilderness experience.

Mount Independence was named by the soldiers who were stationed there when they received word of the signing of the Declaration of Independence, though it is really a rocky bluff at the end of a peninsula, not a mountain. It is located on the narrow southern part of Lake Champlain across from Fort Ticonderoga in New York. To hike through this active archeological site is to step back in time, as you try to imagine what life must have been like here as a soldier.

Mount Independence has four hiking trails, designated by color and ranging from 0.6 mile to 2.5 miles in length. The loop described here heads toward the point on the Blue Trail and returns through the center

Queen Anne's lace

of the peninsula along the highest promontory on the Orange Trail. Maps of the entire trail system are available inside the visitor center.

From the visitor center, bear right up the mowed slope, past a funky hollow maple trunk that looks like a ragged wizard's hat. The lawn is a former military road that used to traverse a treeless military camp. Today, it is a picnic area surrounded by dense forest and an incredible display of wildflowers.

After passing a flagpole that still flies a Colonial flag, turn left at the trailhead sign, following the Red and Blue Trails along the tree line and into the woods. The trail immediately clears the trees again onto another lawn-path, the site of the general hospital. The Red Trail departs to the left. Continue straight ahead on the Blue Trail, reentering the woods on a dirt road.

The road descends through a mixed hardwood forest. It drops steadily to a split-log bridge over a small trickle, then continues downhill at a much shallower grade. Soon, the trail flattens completely, paralleling the shoreline. After a small rise, it follows the edge of a clearing filled with Queen Anne's lace.

At the far corner of the field, the trail reenters the woods, then immediately turns left, passing a murky pool nearly obscured by the trees at the base of the old parapet. The pool was built as a reservoir when

Mount Independence was fortified during the Revolutionary War. Your dog may want to take a dip, but the water is stagnant. Hold him back in anticipation of a better spot ahead.

After a quick glimpse of the shore, the trail swings right up a hill, then bends left past a pile of stones, the site of a quarry dating back to the 1750s when the French controlled the area. Stone from this quarry was hauled over the ice to build Carillon, the original name of Fort Ticonderoga.

The trail parallels the remains of a stone wall on the right. It undulates along to the next clearing where a tool forge used to be located.

At 2.2 miles the Blue Trail ends at the Orange Trail, which drops to a clearing. Bear left at the clearing to a rocky perch, believed to be the place where masts were lowered onto ships. This is a tricky spot for a dog, requiring a hop over a large tree and up a small, but sheer rock. To avoid the scramble, use an alternate path on the right side of the perch. It is also steep, but not rocky. Or have a friend hold your dog while you take a peek. The view across Lake Champlain to Fort Ticonderoga is excellent.

From here, continue on the Orange Trail into the woods along the lake. The trail rounds a bend, then comes to an intersection. Turn left, staying nearest the lake to reach the only easy access to the water. A broad rock slab marks the site where a floating bridge used to connect Mount Independence with Fort Ticonderoga. Your dog will surely go swimming here if he likes the water.

The trail soon reaches another clearing where a stone monument commemorates the naming of Mount Independence. Bear right out of the clearing, immediately arriving at an intersection. Go straight, following the Return Trail sign.

The Orange Trail climbs gently through a cedar grove, then bends away from the point, heading inland. At the next two intersections, turn right toward Horseshoe Battery, where there is a panoramic view of the lake to the north and Fort Ticonderoga. Returning to the last intersection, go straight. The path continues through peaceful woods to another clearing filled with wildflowers, once the location of the central parade-ground. At the other end of the clearing, cross over old log planking and reenter the woods.

A maintenance road merges from the right, then the trail comes to a T. Turn right, taking a short spur to the site where a huge crane was used to lift cannons from the field about 200 feet below. Only the crane's foundation remains today in the shadow of tall cedars, but the site affords another excellent view, this time across the lake to the hills beyond.

Retracing your steps, head straight through the intersection, crossing the maintenance road. The trail becomes a footpath again, although it is wide, smooth, and road-like.

From the next grassy area it is an easy stroll down a wide, grassy road back to the visitor center.

49. Mount Philo

Round trip: 2 miles
Hiking time: 2 hours
High point: 980 feet
Elevation gain: 650 feet
Difficulty: 1 paw (easy)
Fees and permits: $2.50 adults, $2 children ages 4–13
Pet policy: Pets must be leashed; must show proof of rabies vaccination
Map: USGS Mount Philo Quad
Location: Mount Philo State Park; Charlotte, VT
Contact: Vermont Agency of Natural Resources, Department of Forests, Parks & Recreation, 802-425-2390 (seasonal) or 802-786-0060 (off-season), *www.vtstateparks.com*

Getting there: From Route 7 in Charlotte, turn onto State Road just south of the ferry to New York. State Road ends at the parking area and ranger booth at the bottom of the mountain, which is the entrance to Mount Philo State Park.

Mount Philo is the centerpiece of Mount Philo State Park, Vermont's oldest state park. It was established in 1924 when Frances Humphreys gave 150 acres to the state. The hiking trails were added much later, in 1996, by the Vermont Youth Conservation Corps.

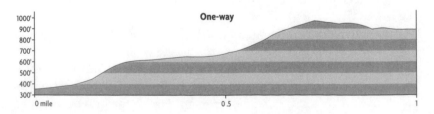

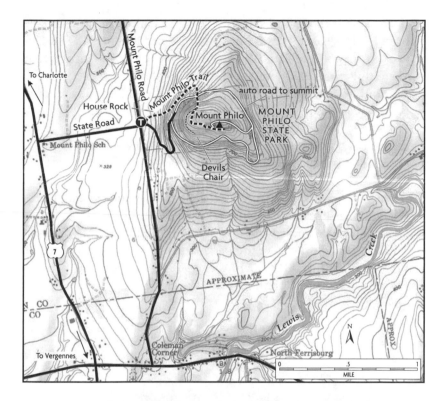

Mount Philo is a midget by normal mountain standards, but it towers over the middle of the Lake Champlain Valley, offering exceptional views of the lake and the Adirondacks beyond. The hike gets an "easy" rating because it is short and low, but it is not wimpy.

The Mount Philo Trail (blue blazes) enters the woods on the left side of the park road, which also goes to the summit. Wildflowers line the path. There are many maples in the hardwood mix, making this hike a local favorite during fall foliage season. The park is open from mid-May through mid-October. Do not stray from the path, as there is poison ivy throughout the woods, and not just on the ground. Some of the woody vines are old, but still potent.

The trail climbs steadily to House Rock, a large boulder that is hollowed out underneath, like an overhang. The trail turns left around House Rock, then traverses to the northeast. It squeezes between a tree and a large rock as it climbs again, passing a couple of other big boulders.

At 0.4 mile the trail bends sharply right, then meets the auto road. The path continues across the road and slightly downhill, leaving the road by wooden stairs. It climbs to a short rise, where a narrow, rocky spur exits right to Devils Chair. Devils Chair, a rock formed like a chair, is rather unexciting for you and your dog, although the 0.1 mile approach to it is interesting, particularly walking under the "leaner" (one large rock leaning on another). The intersection is notable itself for the cleft in the rock that is fun to squeeze inside.

From here, the trail continues uphill, swinging right at the top of another distinct boulder, where there is an obstructed view through cedar trees of Lake Champlain and the farmland below. The trail bends back around the cliff to the left, then heads upward again, becoming rather rough and steep. At about 0.8 mile, the pitch eases and the trail bends to the right, passing a rock perch. The perch is worth a peek. This time the panorama is unblocked and breathtaking.

The trail bends away from the perch and climbs another rise to the summit picnic area and the open, rocky peak. On a clear day, you can see as far as Whiteface Mountain near Lake Placid, New York.

Mount Philo

NORTHEAST KINGDOM

50. Bald Mountain

Round trip: 4 miles

Hiking time: 3 hours

High point: 3315 feet

Elevation gain: 1450 feet

Difficulty: 2 paws (moderate)

Pet policy: Pets must be leashed or under immediate control of owners

Maps: USGS Island Pond Quad; Westmore Association Trail Map (available free to hikers at Westmore Town Clerk's office, White Caps store, Northern Exposure store, and Willowood Camp Grounds)

Location: Westmore, VT

Contact: Vermont Department of Forests, Parks & Recreation, 802-751-0110, *www.state.vt.us/anr;* Westmore Association Trail Committee, email: *paulmoffat@aol.com* (no telephone or website)

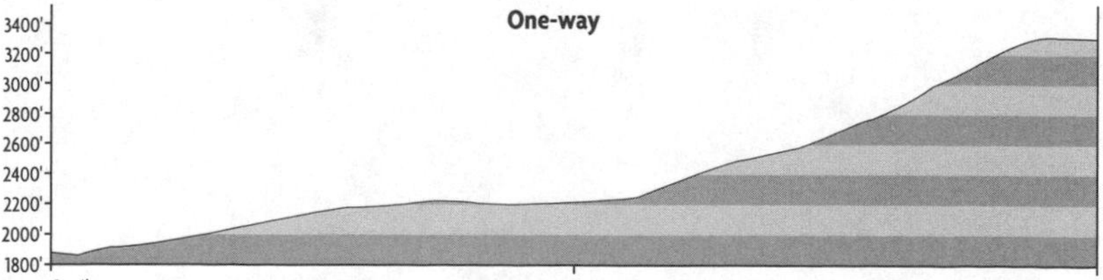

Getting there: Follow Route 5A along the shore of Lake Willoughby (see map for Hike 52). In Westmore, turn onto Long Pond Road. The trailhead

and a small parking area are on the left, 0.1 mile after the boat access on Long Pond. Please do not block the gate.

Don't let the name fool you. There are at least five Bald Mountains in Vermont, none of which have bald summits, but their tops were once clear as a result of forest fires. Subsequent erosion left the peaks bald for many years, but gradually the hardiest plants returned, followed by trees again. Bald Mountain in Westmore is not only the tallest Bald Mountain in Vermont, it is also the tallest peak in the Lake Willoughby area. Its fire tower is a great destination for hikers. Dogs will enjoy the exercise it takes to get there and the chance to explore the summit clearing and rustic shelter, where there are many interesting things to sniff.

The Long Pond–Bald Mountain Trail departs from Long Pond Road and is described here because, of the two routes up the mountain, it is the easiest to find and has the best parking. The trail begins on an old logging

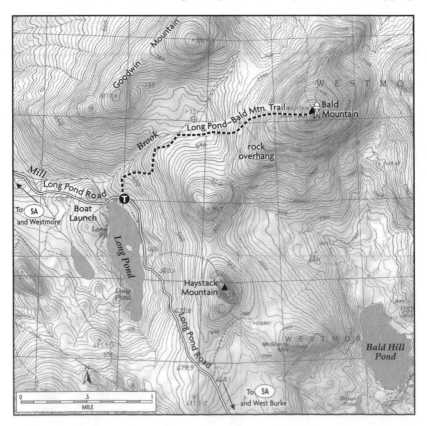

Cleo soaks her paws on the way up Bald Mountain.

road that is now as much grass as gravel. At the first fork, bear right (east). A sign on a tree says "Trail," with an arrow underneath it pointing to the right. A short way later, in a small clearing, the trail forks again. Bear right again at the end of the clearing. A few minutes later, the trail bends left into the woods and flattens, becoming more footpath than road. Blue blazes appear on the trees. The path traverses slightly downhill through a deciduous forest with a full canopy overhead. The many maple trees make this section a colorful area during the fall foliage season.

At about 1 mile the trail crosses a streamlet, the first of several stream crossings, none of which are reliable. If you find water, let your dog take her time, as the next streambed might be dry. After three consecutive stream crossings, the climb steepens slightly. After another small stream crossing and a series of log steps, the trail meanders through the woods on its long approach to the mountain. About ten minutes later, the uphill climb starts in earnest, passing over a split-log bridge, then through a couple of short switchbacks before taking a more direct line up the slope. The footing remains relatively good, although more roots now crisscross the trail.

At about 1.7 miles the trail bends left (northeast), passing an impressive rock overhang, about four feet high and fifteen feet long, as if a giant wedge had been taken out of the mountainside. A root from a birch tree grows down and the trunk of another tree grows up, like two pillars in front of the shallow cave.

Above the overhang, the trail climbs more sharply through spruce trees, immediately passing an odd hole on the right. It crosses a tangle of roots and slab, before reaching a short, but hefty single-log bridge. The log crosses a narrow rock chasm, about a foot across and six feet deep. Your dog will leap it without a thought.

From there it is a short, steady climb to the summit. The fire tower has been restored by volunteers from the North Woods Stewardship Center, the Northeast section of the Green Mountain Club, and the Westmore Association. The view from the tower is impressive on a clear day. (Leave your dog tied near the base while you check out the view; it is not safe for dogs to climb the fire tower.) To the south, Bald Hill Pond (close) and Newark Pond (farther) point toward Burke Mountain. The north end of Lake Willoughby is visible to the west, over the right shoulder of Haystack Mountain. Beyond Haystack, you can see Mount Pisgah, then Mount Hor, on either side of Lake Willoughby. The cliffs beyond belong to Wheeler Mountain. Several peaks in Quebec lie to the north across Lake Memphremagog. And the towering Presidential Range in New Hampshire lies on the southeastern horizon.

Note: Only the very top of Bald Mountain is on state land. The rest of the hike is on private property. The owners live nearby and ask hikers to leave no trace and respect their land. No overnight camping or campfires are permitted.

51. Jay Peak

Round trip: 3.2 miles (3.7 miles including loop to Jay Camp)
Hiking time: 3 hours
High point: 3861 feet
Elevation gain: 1680 feet
Difficulty: 2 paws (moderate)
Map: USGS Jay Peak Quad
Location: Jay State Forest; Jay, VT
Contact: Green Mountain Club, 802-244-7037, *www.greenmountain club.org;* Vermont Department of Forests, Parks & Recreation, 802-751-0110, *www.state.vt.us/anr*

Getting there: Take Route 242 southeast of the Jay Peak Ski Area to a height of land known as Jay Pass. Watch for the turnout on the left, which is the best parking. The Long Trail crosses the road at this point, but there is no obvious sign. Put your pooch on a leash to cross the road from the turnout on Route 242 to the trailhead. The road is not usually

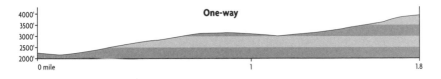

busy, but the few cars that pass might not expect pedestrians, particularly since the Long Trail (LT) is unmarked at this crossing.

Jay Peak is the northernmost peak in Vermont of any prominence. It is most known as a ski resort, but hikers enjoy it for its views to Canada, only 10 miles away. Dogs will find most of the route rather easy, with one exception, where the Long Trail (LT) crosses a ski trail.

The trail enters the woods on the LT north (white blazes), immediately passing the Atlas Valley Shelter, a four-man lean-to built in 1967 from wood supplied by the Atlas timber company. It was not intended for overnight use, but it works in a pinch.

The trail starts out as much stream as footpath after a heavy rain, but the footing is easy. It soon begins to climb, getting increasingly steeper and becoming more rocky and well-worn.

At 0.1 mile, the Jay Loop (blue blazes) to Jay Camp leaves to the left (west). A flat, wet 0.3 mile from the trailhead, Jay Camp is a cabin maintained by the Green Mountain Club, and a much better choice than the minute Atlas Valley Shelter for those wishing to spend the night. Constructed in 1958, Jay Camp sleeps eight to twelve people and has a reliable spring about fifty feet away. The Jay Loop swings back toward the main trail to the right of the cabin, rejoining it about 0.4 mile from the trailhead.

Between the south and north ends of the Jay Loop, the main trail climbs stiffly until it passes a large old birch tree, devoid of low paper bark. Its roots form a lump in the trail, and its double trunk leans out to the left over the hillside. The trail swings around this odd tree and continues to climb, now at a more moderate rate, in a generally northwesterly direction. It does not have switchbacks per se, just arcing turns. At about 0.6 mile the softwoods start to intrude. The trail eases, winding through a berry patch. (Watch the prickers along the side of the trail!) The grade remains easy as the berry bushes give way to ferns, and evergreens take over. At about 0.8 mile, there is a break in the trees to the left with a view of the neighboring peaks to the north and into Canada.

Around the next bend the path gets steeper again, crossing short

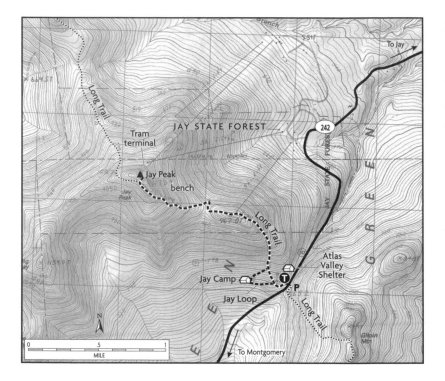

sections of slab and climbing up a number of stone steps. Nothing is extreme to this point, and all is easy for a dog to negotiate. However, the upper part of the climb is more challenging. Soon the spruce trees close in as the trail begins a longer, more sustained climb, crossing sections of rough slab and rock. The trail makes a sharp left just below a ski trail, noticeable mainly because of the snowmaking pipes that run along the ground above the turn. After that, the slabs lengthen and can be slippery. At 1.4 miles, the LT meets a ski trail at the ski area boundary. This is the trickiest section of the hike for a dog, as he must get over two snowmaking pipes, which are surrounded by large rocks. Guide your dog toward the downhill cut in the fence for the easiest crossing.

From here, you can either turn left, following the ski trail to the summit, or cross the ski trail, continuing on the LT, which heads up a rocky ridge parallel to the ski trail. The LT is more interesting. It goes over a rocky hump, then climbs steadily toward the summit cone, passing a polished stone bench, just below the tram terminal at 1.6 miles.

Most hikers with dogs prefer to stop at the polished bench, away from the tourists around the tram. The bench is inscribed with the words, "A place to sit, a place to be, a place to appreciate all that we see." And there is certainly a lot to see. To the south, you can look down the spine of the Green Mountains as far as Camels Hump. The White Mountains and the Adirondacks are visible to the southeast and southwest, respectively. To the north lies the Sutton Range in Quebec. The large lake to the northeast is Lake Memphremagog, which straddles the Canadian border.

Jewelweed (Spotted Touch-Me-Not) by Jay Camp

52. Mount Pisgah

Round trip: 3.4 miles
Hiking time: 3 hours
High point: 2751 feet
Elevation gain: 1450 feet
Difficulty: 2 paws (moderate)
Pet policy: Pets must be leashed or under control
Map: USGS Sutton Quad
Location: By Lake Willoughby, between West Burke and Westmore, VT
Contact: Vermont Department of Forests, Parks & Recreation,
     802-751-0110, *www.state.vt.us/anr;* Westmore Association Trail
     Committee, email: *paulmoffat@aol.com* (no telephone or website)

Getting there: Take Route 5A north from West Burke (or south from
Westmore). The trailhead is just south of Lake Willoughby on the east
side of the road, marked by a sign, "Willoughby State Forest Trailhead."
Best parking is at the trailhead, with additional parking across the street
at the trailhead for Mount Hor.

Mount Pisgah lives up to the biblical origin of its name—the mountain
where Moses viewed the Promised Land. At least, it offers views of biblical proportions. Mount Pisgah defines the eastern wall of Willoughby
Gap on the eastern side of Lake Willoughby, a landlocked fjord that is
both a National Natural Landmark and a designated natural area by the
State of Vermont. The lake is the centerpiece of 7300-acre Willoughby
State Forest, which was established in 1928. It is sometimes called "the
Lucerne of America" for its shape and the way the mountains on either
side of its shores rise so steeply.

   The hike up Mount Pisgah offers some spectacular views of the lake,
but it is not a great choice if you are scared of heights, or as one fellow

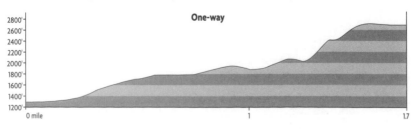

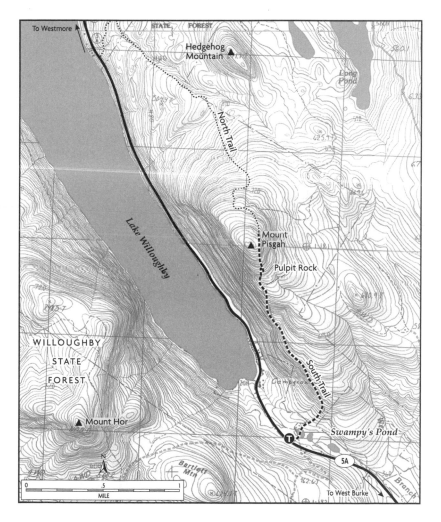

hiker once stated, "Not scared of heights. Scared of edges." Dogs are not acrophobic, so they will not experience an adrenaline rush atop one of Pisgah's precipitous overlooks, yet your pet will like this hike for its smooth footing and the chance to swim in the sizable beaver pond near the trailhead, known as Swampy's Pond.

The South Trail starts out tamely enough, crossing the beaver pond. The trail bends around the pond through a mixed forest of hemlock, birch, and maple, giving the area an Adirondack feel. It remains relatively flat as it winds past moss-covered boulders that seem to have been thrown at random throughout the woods.

At 0.4 mile the trail turns left and begins climbing steadily. It remains wide with good footing and is in excellent condition thanks to a local youth group from Westmore who spend their summers on the trail crew here.

There are numerous glimpses of the lake and Mount Hor, the western wall of Willoughby Gap, through the trees as you ascend past a section with rough-hewn handrails. The first clear overlook is slightly farther, over a hedge of low cedars. Watch your step and keep your dog on a short leash. It is a big drop.

At 0.9 mile Pulpit Rock bulges from the cliff, offering an unobstructed view of the entire lake, the cliffs to the right, Mount Hor across the gap, and a small marina 650 feet below. Use caution with your dog by every lookout, but especially this one. If you are hiking with another person, have your partner hold your dog on a leash while you check out the cliff-side scenery. Stay low to get closer to the edge, but still give it a lot of respect. There are no guardrails here.

Above Pulpit Rock the trail bends right, away from the cliff area, and flattens out for a short stretch. As it begins to climb again, check out the large boulders on the right, which were actually one boulder until it broke apart. Today it looks like a huge 3-D puzzle waiting to be put back together.

The trail climbs more moderately as it winds back toward the lake. It passes through a birch grove and dips over a single-log bridge, which is optional, as the path is perfectly fine next to it and the preferable route for your canine companion.

The trail becomes rougher and rockier before turning away from the lake again. At 1.7 miles it climbs up a rock slab to open rock amidst the scrub trees. The word "trail" with an arrow pointing both north and south is painted in yellow on the rock. While technically not above tree line and not the summit, this open area is close enough, roomy enough for a summit picnic, and offers views to the south toward Burke Mountain, Newark Pond, and even the White Mountains on a clear day.

The real summit is a few steps farther, unmarked, in the trees. There are additional overlooks as you traverse the summit ridge. After you have seen your fill, return the way you came.

Opposite: Bridge across Swampy's Pond on the approach to Mount Pisgah

CONTACTS AND ADDITIONAL RESOURCES

Dog Gear
Ruff Wear
888-783-3932
www.ruffwear.com

Human Gear/Apparel
Mountain Hardwear
800-953-8375
www.mountainhardwear.com

Dog-Friendly Naturalists and Guide Services
Killington Resort Hiking Center
802-422-6200
www.killington.com

Mad River Glen Naturalist Program
802-496-3551
www.madriverglen.com

Emergency Assistance
New Hampshire or Vermont State Police
Dial 9-1-1
800-525-5555

AMC Pinkham Notch Visitor Center
603-466-2725

Green Mountain Club Headquarters
877-484-5053 (after calling 9-1-1)

Nature Books
Carter, Kate. *Wildflowers of Vermont.* Waterbury Center: Cotton Brook
    Publications, 2001.

Little, Elbert Luther. *National Audubon Society Field Guide to North American Trees – Eastern Region*. New York: Alfred Knopf, 1980.

Thieret, John W., William A. Niering, and Nancy C. Olmstead. *National Audubon Society Field Guide to North American Wildflowers – Eastern Region*, Revised edition. New York: Alfred Knopf, 2001.

Guidebooks

Daniell, Gene and Steven D. Smith (editors), *AMC White Mountain Guide: Hiking Trails in the White Mountain National Forest*, 27th edition. Boston: Appalachian Mountain Club, 2003.

Dickerman, Mike and Steven D. Smith. *The 4000-Footers of the White Mountains: A Guide and History*. Littleton: Bondcliff Books, 2001.

Gange, Jared. *Hiker's Guide to the Mountains of New Hampshire: Classic Hikes of the White Mountains - 200 Best Hikes in New Hampshire*, 2nd edition. Burlington: Huntington Graphics, 2002.

Gange, Jared. *Hiker's Guide to the Mountains of Vermont*, 3rd edition. Burlington: Huntington Graphics, 2001.

Green Mountain Club. *50 Hikes in Vermont: Walks, Hikes, and Overnights in the Green Mountain State*, 6th Edition. Rutland: Green Mountain Club, 2003.

Green Mountain Club. *Day Hiker's Guide to Vermont*, 4th edition. Rutland: Green Mountain Club, 2002.

Green Mountain Club. *The Long Trail Guide: Hiking Vermont's High Ridge*, 25th edition. Rutland: Green Mountain Club, 2003.

Lewis, Cynthia C. and Thomas J. *Best Hikes with Children: Vermont, New Hampshire & Maine*, 2nd edition. Seattle: The Mountaineers Books, 2000.

Monadnock-Sunapee Greenway Trail Club. *Monadnock-Sunapee Greenway Trail Guide*, 6th edition. Tilton: Sant Bani Press, 2001.

INDEX

ABOUT THE AUTHOR

Lisa Densmore is an Emmy© award–winning television host and producer who specializes in outdoor, sports, and adventure programming. She has covered hiking and camping topics for PBS, RSN, and OLN. She is currently the co-host and a field producer for "Wildlife Journal," which airs on PBS stations in Vermont, New Hampshire, and Maine, and a freelance writer. She has published hundreds of articles in both trade and consumer magazines, many on hiking in Vermont and New Hampshire. A graduate of Dartmouth College and a lifetime member of the Dartmouth Outing Club, Lisa has spent the last thirty years hiking the trails in the twin states, as well as throughout the United States, Europe, and other parts of the world. A lifelong dog-lover and the owner of two Chesapeake Bay retrievers, she is rarely in the woods without one or both of her brown furry friends. This is Lisa's second book. Her first, *Ski Faster*, was published in 1999 by McGraw-Hill.

Lisa with Bravo on Brownsville Rock (Mount Ascutney, Hike 38)

THE MOUNTAINEERS, founded in 1906, is a nonprofit outdoor activity and conservation club, whose mission is "to explore, study, preserve, and enjoy the natural beauty of the outdoors. . . . " Based in Seattle, Washington, the club is now the third-largest such organization in the United States, with seven branches throughout Washington State.

The Mountaineers sponsors both classes and year-round outdoor activities in the Pacific Northwest, which include hiking, mountain climbing, ski-touring, snowshoeing, bicycling, camping, kayaking, nature study, sailing, and adventure travel. The club's conservation division supports environmental causes through educational activities, sponsoring legislation, and presenting informational programs.

All club activities are led by skilled, experienced instructors, who are dedicated to promoting safe and responsible enjoyment and preservation of the outdoors.

If you would like to participate in these organized outdoor activities or the club's programs, consider a membership in The Mountaineers. For information and an application, write or call The Mountaineers, Club Headquarters, 300 Third Avenue West, Seattle, WA 98119; 206-284-6310. You can also visit the club's website at www.mountaineers.org or contact The Mountaineers via email at clubmail@mountaineers.org.

The Mountaineers Books, an active, nonprofit publishing program of the club, produces guidebooks, instructional texts, historical works, natural history guides, and works on environmental conservation. All books produced by The Mountaineers Books fulfill the club's mission.

Send or call for our catalog of more than 500 outdoor titles:

The Mountaineers Books
1001 SW Klickitat Way, Suite 201
Seattle, WA 98134
800-553-4453
mbooks@mountaineersbooks.org
www.mountaineersbooks.org

The Mountaineers Books is proud to be a corporate sponsor of The Leave No Trace Center for Outdoor Ethics, whose mission is to promote and inspire responsible outdoor recreation through education, research, and partnerships. The Leave No Trace program is focused specifically on human-powered (nonmotorized) recreation.

Leave No Trace strives to educate visitors about the nature of their recreational impacts, as well as offer techniques to prevent and minimize such impacts. Leave No Trace is best understood as an educational and ethical program, not as a set of rules and regulations.

For more information, visit *www.LNT.org,* or call 800-332-4100.

OTHER TITLES YOU MIGHT ENJOY FROM
THE MOUNTAINEERS BOOKS

Best Hikes with Children in Vermont, New Hampshire & Maine, 2nd Edition,
Cynthia Copeland & Thomas Lewis
Short hikes for short legs, as well as advice for parents on keeping the kids engaged and helping them learn to love the outdoors.

Northern Forest Canoe Trail Maps
Trail section 4: Islands and Farms: Vermont, Lake Champlain to Missisquoi River
Trail section 6: Northeast Kingdom: Vermont/Quebec, Lake Memphremagog to Connecticut River
Trail section 7: Great North Woods: New Hampshire, Connecticut River to Umbagog Lake
Waterproof paddling maps to the area's ancient liquid highway—the 740-mile Northern Forest Canoe Trail.

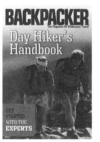

Day Hiker's Handbook: Get Started with the Experts,
Michael Lanza
For beginning hikers—choosing gear, finding partners, handling dangers, and more.

Conditioning for Outdoor Fitness: Functional Exercise & Nutrition for Every Body, 2nd Edition,
David Musnick, M.D., and Mark Pierce, A.T.C.
Illustrated step-by-step fitness training for a wide variety of outdoor activities